W9-AAY-818

CONTENTS

Leaving Laodicea

"*Leaving Laodicea* was not just written, but rather birthed out of revelation, anguish, travail and tears. These pages came through hours of meditation, prayer and waiting upon God for His heart to be revealed concerning His Church.

"Every pastor, Christian worker and professing believer should read this book. It's time for the Church to awaken out of her spiritual lethargy, shake off her grave clothes and allow the Spirit of God to prepare her for her eternal role — that of a pure and passionate Bride."

David Ravenhill
Teacher and author of *For God's Sake, Grow Up*
Lindale, Texas

"Jeanne Terrell strips the veneer off of our comfortable Christian existence, exposing it for what it often is — a complacent life. The good news is that she doesn't leave us there. *Leaving Laodicea* is a life-giving roadmap to the heart of God and to the passionate life He gives to those who earnestly seek Him."

Ted Haggard
Senior Pastor, New Life Church
Colorado Springs, Colorado

"With a pen in hand and tearstained cheeks, Jeanne Terrell calls for the radical transformation of the Church. If you are ready for an exodus from the flatlands of lukewarm living, *Leaving Laodicea* will stir up within you a holy passion for the journey. Read it and prepare to pack your bags."

Terry Crist
Senior Pastor, CitiChurch International
Author of *Learning the Language of Babylon*
Scottsdale, Arizona

"This book will help to lead us out of the lukewarm 'Laodicean Church' and help us go forward into the divine move of the 'Fire of God,' until we believe and are inspired to walk into the high calling of God in Christ Jesus."

Dr. Fuchsia T. Pickett
Teacher and author of fourteen books, including *Worship Him*
Blountsville, Tennessee

"**Gripping!** This book, *Leaving Laodicea*, is for the hungry. This book could not have come at a more important time … . Jeanne's practical application brings this revelation to everyday life. The principles in this book are thought-provoking, significant and immediately applicable. This book is a manual for those who desire to walk out their hunger for God in everyday living."

Sam Hinn
Senior Pastor, The Gathering Place
Author of *Changed in His Presence*
Lake Mary, Florida

"*Leaving Laodicea* is a clarion call to awaken the Body of Christ out of her lukewarm state of apathetic 'churchianity,' to truly become salt and light to this present generation. Read this book, and you just might be the next one awakened from slumber into passionate, relational Christianity."

Jim W. Goll
Ministry to the Nations
Author of *The Lost Art of Intercession*
Franklin, Tennessee

"*Leaving Laodicea* is a powerful and startling 'Behold, I stand at the door and knock!' for the modern Church. This book captures the heart of God toward us in this hour! I urge the reader to prayerfully read and reflect on the message of this book. The Spirit of God is poised to address important places in your own heart through the exhortations of this book! If you have ears to hear, this message will draw you into renewed passion and intimacy with the Lover of your soul!"

Steven Carpenter
Director of the Forerunner School of Prayer
Kansas City, Missouri

Leaving Laodicea

A Call to Spiritual Passion

by

Jeanne Terrell

McDougal Publishing is a ministry of The McDougal Foundation, Inc., a Maryland nonprofit corporation dedicated to spreading the Gospel of the Lord Jesus Christ to as many people as possible in the shortest time possible.

Published by:

McDougal Publishing
P.O. Box 3595
Hagerstown, MD 21742-3595
www.mcdougalpublishing.com

ISBN 1-58158-040-1

Printed in the United States of America
For Worldwide Distribution

FOREWORD

Aren't you amazed at the mercy of God? He always demonstrates such love toward us, even when we just aren't listening! How many of us are truly patient when we must repeat ourselves over and over to our children? Yet, it seems that whenever the Lord has something important to say to us, He is willing to use a multitude of avenues to get our attention and communicate His message to us.

There's no doubt about it. Jesus is resolute to awaken holy passion in His bride. He is replaying His desire for us over and over again. He has received a welcomed response from some, and none from others. But He is not easily discouraged, and His efforts have not diminished in the least. His voice is only getting louder and more insistent. The stronger and more persistent He becomes, the harder He is to ignore! The Lord has a divine strategy, fueled by His incredible passion for us.

This book is a heart cry from the Lord to His Church, and we need to soberly receive the warnings that go along with it. Jeanne has been given a unique and passionate message from the Lord that will indeed be hard to ignore. The Laodicean Church, admonished by Jesus Christ in Revelation 3:14-22, clearly mirrors many of the attributes of today's Church. We have become self-sufficient and callous, wandering far from His ways and far from full devotion to Him. Even as many of us believe that we sincerely have responded to His passionate love, corporately we live in a perpetual state of lukewarmness. That should grieve us even if we are not blatantly guilty ourselves, realizing that the Lord is worshiped only halfheartedly by many who are part of His Bride.

Ironically, this is a time when the Lord is pouring out His power as never before in modern history. Churches now living in "Laodicea" are on a dangerous course if they will not forsake her. Not only do we need an escape from this lethargic stronghold, but we desperately need to be convinced that He is calling us into a deeper intimacy with Himself that is simply unimaginable.

All over the world, "prophetic wooings" are surfacing — and they are not all coming from the usual or expected places. Some are coming through the hearts of those who, like Mary of Bethany, have sat at His feet, out of the limelight. Those Marys have been intent on the Lord, hearing His secret whispers and letting His heart cries become their own.

The Lord doesn't always call a Mary to speak out, but when He does, she will carry the anointing of one who has been with Jesus. Therefore, we would all do well to open our hearts and listen. A true Mary has a real burden to drive others to the feet of Jesus, not just tell them what she knows; she wants others to hear the truth she has heard and to see the beauty of what she has seen for themselves.

So, while reading this book, I would encourage you to do the following: First, listen for truth. When it grabs hold of you, take it to the altar and let Him consume anything lukewarm in your life. Then, be expectant for a fresh glimpse of the beauty of the Lord Jesus that you haven't seen before. When you catch one, pursue it with all your heart and let it take you to His feet — far from Laodicea.

Mike Bickle
Director of International House of Prayer
Kansas City, Missouri

And to the angel of the church of the Laodiceans write,
"These things says the Amen, the Faithful and True Witness,
the Beginning of the creation of God:

'I know your works, that you are neither cold nor hot.
I could wish you were cold or hot.

'So then, because you are lukewarm, and neither cold nor hot,
I will vomit you out of My mouth.

'Because you say, "I am rich, have become wealthy, and have
need of nothing" — and do not know that you are wretched,
miserable, poor, blind, and naked —

'I counsel you to buy from Me gold refined in the fire, that
you may be rich; and white garments , that you may be clothed,
that the shame of your nakedness may not be revealed; and
anoint your eyes with eye salve, that you may see.

'As many as I love, I rebuke and chasten.
Therefore be zealous and repent.

'Behold, I stand at the door and knock.
If anyone hears My voice and opens the door,
I will come in to him and dine with him, and he with Me.

'To him who overcomes I will grant to sit with Me on My
throne, as I also overcame and sat down with My Father on
His throne.

'He who has an ear, let him hear what the Spirit says to the
churches.'"

—Revelation 3:14-22

INTRODUCTION

"An overwhelming, lukewarm complacency smothered the city like a soft, heavy blanket. The unsuspecting were mysteriously lulled to sleep with symptoms that were inescapable, yet irresistible. In fact, the enemy's success in establishing his stronghold was so astounding and the deception so complete that no one seemed immune. There was an eerie, uncanny unity among the local churches, but it was clearly an evil alliance. A certain glint of pride emanated from those who joined the 'Brotherhood of the Lukewarm' ...."

No, you are not trapped on the pages of an imitation Frank Peretti novel. In fact, this scenario is not meant to be fictitious. Unfortunately, it is much closer to reality that you might imagine. There was a church in a real city — Laodicea — which was addressed in the book of Revelation and was deemed "lukewarm" by Jesus Himself. However, the spiritual implications and correlations to today's Church are absolutely inescapable. So, come to think of it, maybe you *are* trapped!

Several years ago, *I* was feeling trapped. There was a point in my life when I knew that I was being engaged in spiritual warfare, but I wasn't sure where the attack was coming from or even what I needed to battle against. In my struggle to maintain the presence of God in my life, I was met with a strange vacuum that would try to deprive me of any spiritual desire whatsoever. The residual aftermath was a tormenting feeling of emptiness — my "punishment," enforced by an enemy who wanted to prevent me from seeking the Lord. Reviving my secret relationship with the Lord was difficult, and when I felt I had finally regained ground, maintaining it was even harder. After a while, I began to condemn myself. Not knowing the source, I concluded that this was some small thing that should easily be overcome.

I was confronted with the possibility that I was a "spiritual pig." In the past, I had been blessed by wonderful ministries and perhaps even spoiled by the privileges I had enjoyed as a believer. Our family had recently moved to a different geographic area, and I wondered if the Lord had "banished" me to a place of inferior spiritual amenities on purpose. There was no magnificent feeding trough. Had I gathered impartations, teachings, revelations and other "manna" from the spiritually gifted, only to become self-absorbed on such a rich diet?

My weaknesses and failures were magnified — I had no spiritual crutches, and I felt all alone. Most of all, I was disgusted that my relationship with the Lord had apparently been that shallow. In the past, I had devoted myself wholeheartedly to worship, and the Holy Spirit had become my most treasured friend. But now, I wasn't sure what had transpired. Could it be that all the time I had thought I was growing in the Lord, the devil himself was fattening me for the slaughter?

For some reason, I didn't see this as a problem that was originated by my enemy. My own spiritual character was in question. After all, wasn't I indeed weaker than I thought? If not, I should prove it by rebuking this and moving on without breaking stride. My soul was being persecuted by something that even tried to blame me for my obvious lack of power over it.

As I sat in that pit of despair kicking myself, there was a natural tendency to be ashamed to ask the mighty, omnipotent Lord to answer my silly questions. I felt guilty and unworthy. I struggled, trying to find the calm assurance that His compassion would reach my most idiotic dilemma. But James 1:5 says, *"If any of you lacks wisdom, let him ask of God, who gives to all liberally."* Somehow, I grappled and asked Him to show me what was happening to me, and He rescued me with His answer.

He conveyed to me that even if I were the hottest drop of oil imaginable, being dropped into a bucket of lukewarm water would put me in the midst of trouble. Not only would I be too small to change the temperature of the water, but my environment would be working against me until I conformed to it. Soon, I would be lukewarm too. The Lord Himself had allowed me to be dropped into a lukewarm spiritual climate, and pressure was being exerted on me to adapt to that atmosphere. That was my warfare.

I then realized something wonderful. It was actually a good thing that I was miserable. I despised what was happening to me, and that was an indication that I was resisting it. I was not cozy under this lukewarm blanket, and I had been blindly trying to fight my way out.

With this realization, my passion for the Lord began to be renewed again. It returned because I ran to Him, knowing He was the only refuge from what prevailed around me. Even though some fruit came into my life as a result, I began to wonder why this ordeal had been necessary. After all, on the down side, I was experiencing a profound lack of fellowship and significant participation in a local body. Yet I became consumed with seeking revelation about how to seal the demise of anything lukewarm in my life. I had gained strength, but I wanted victory. Also, I had a horrifying thought — that those most influenced by lukewarm tendencies were often the most oblivious to it. Then, I wondered how many other people had found themselves in predicaments like mine, yet were unable to grasp the wisdom they needed to oppose it.

I began to study Revelation 3:14-22 with a fervor. I was familiar with the message to the Laodicean church, but it suddenly held more personal meaning for me. The deepest impact came when I was reminded that Laodicea was given the opportunity for a higher blessing than any of the other six churches that Jesus addressed in Revelation — those who were deemed to be overcomers in that city would be invited to sit with Jesus on His throne! This is the highest level of intimacy possible with the Lord, and obviously, the attainment of a higher reward would engage a more difficult opposition to overcome. No wonder there was such a battle for me in this Laodicea!

It was apparent that the Lord had granted me a tremendous eye-opening opportunity. I came to see to a greater extent that *we all live in Laodicea*, especially with the abundance of blessings we enjoy in the Western world. In my case, I did love the Lord and had a close relationship with Him. It was true that I had been blessed by sitting under some incredible ministries, which encouraged me and kept my spiritual passion high. When He placed me in "lesser" spiritual circumstances, it accentuated the lukewarm effects in my own life and introduced me to the once-hidden enemy that I still face every day. I felt the crashing reality that this was how most of the Body of Christ lives, without even realizing that there is much more.

It has been said that if we could have one peek of hell, we would never forget to work out our salvation with fear and trembling. We'd preach to every person and would not be so prone to sin. Having taken a peek into Laodicea, everything in me wants to flee and take everybody with me. But unfortunately, I now realize that I live there. You live there too. We must recognize that. If we do, then we can also be encouraged that we don't have to submit to the governing forces there. In our hearts, we *can* leave Laodicea.

It is frequently observed that when the Lord took the children out of Egypt, He had an awful time getting the Egypt out of *them.* Left to our own devices, we could never decide for the eternal over the temporal. We must all be awakened to the grave consequences of boasting of spiritual wealth when we are, in reality, impoverished in the things of God. And He is the only one who can reveal that to each of us.

Being vomited from the mouth of God seems worse than I can imagine. Not only do I not want to be reduced to a regurgitated glob, but facing that kind of rejection from the One you claim to love the most is heartrending. The mere thought of it should lead us to say, "Lord, try me; refine me for You. Whatever You've got to do, do it." Unfortunately, we are sometimes compelled in a moment to say this without giving true surrender and just weight to our words.

The Lord's heart breaks over lukewarm Christians because He would prefer to draw them to Himself with His lavish love, but they are often so desensitized that they cannot respond in their present condition. Therefore, He may come with a corrective word and bring discipline. But, the *Lord chastises **because** He loves*. We must remember that *He does not love to chastise.* He is just looking for the glorious result.

I pray that what you read in this book will impart a hunger in you to seek the Holy Spirit's empowerment of resolve and strength for the race of an overcomer. The reward of being in the presence of the Lord forever is well worth the laying down of a life. God desires and deserves the undivided hearts of all those who call Him "Lord."

As I sought the Lord for prophetic understanding on this issue, I was overwhelmed with the tidal wave of response from Him. The more I asked, the more I felt He was telling me, "I'm so glad you asked." My personal notes became a manuscript, which sat in a notebook for several years. During that time, an onslaught of popular books was released, touching on spiritual hunger, passion and the "fervently going after God" theme. What has been said has been said very well and has undoubtedly lit a fire in many believers. Over and over, these messages confirmed to me that the things I had already written were truly a priority on the Lord's heart.

It was only the result of an unexpected prophetic word through a friend, Pastor Kevin Kringel (thank you, Kevin) that the Lord convinced me to publish this book. I was stirred up as I visited the manuscript again, and I could only conclude that He is not tiring in His pursuit of a holy bride. He is not finished extending that invitation of intimacy and passion to each of us.

CHAPTER 1

THE LUKEWARM NATURE

t is not surprising that the Lord would use everyday terms to explain profound spiritual truths to the Laodicean church. The Scriptures are full of parables and illustrations that show man the ways of God. Raw spiritual truth would be difficult for human flesh to swallow whole, so the Lord graciously breaks it down into pieces to make it easier to assimilate.

The definition of *lukewarm* is: "moderately warm; tepid; not ardent; indifferent." With few exceptions, something that is lukewarm is not desirable — it carries a negative connotation. For example, foods and beverages are nearly always more palatable when served either hot or cold. Even setting personal taste aside, some foods are not served lukewarm because it can be unhealthful — even fatal — because there is a precarious "mid-range" temperature at which bacteria thrive. Meat and eggs are especially subject to this hazard. Refrigeration or cooking to a high temperature is required to kill harmful organisms and retard spoilage.

This model in the natural world can give us understanding of God's perspective on the church that is *"neither cold nor hot."* What does it mean to be lukewarm? It is interesting that the Bible doesn't have much to say on the subject. In fact, the term appears only once — in Revelation 3:16, in the message to Laodicea.

So if God detests the lukewarm condition, why doesn't He ever go into detail about something that so disturbs Him? Somehow, by His omission, He basically gives no credence to the condition. He is perhaps demonstrating that from Heaven's point of view, there are no gray areas. There is good and evil — nothing else. He does not allow a third, compromising point of view; God deals in absolutes. We may view our own lifestyles and decisions on a sliding scale, but under the magnification of the Holy Spirit, the intentions of our hearts are clearly seen. This is how a "good" man by earthly standards could spend eternity in hell. The Lord's assessments are not harsh or unjust; on the contrary, they are totally righteous, revealing perfect truth.

In the church today, we might use the term "lukewarm" to describe the backslidden Christian, the stuffy, "religious" legalist or even the poor guy who falls asleep in church. We have learned to identify a tepid person by the lack of fervency in his manner. We consider his relationship with the Lord to be blatantly void of the passion that we expect to see in an exuberant follower of Christ.

The tendency to judge a brother by externals should be kept in check, but the Laodicean certainly could have displayed some of these characteristics. The Lord did in fact choose to use His just evaluation of Laodicea as a warning to the body at large. Yet, if we misinterpret the application of this warning, we may be inclined to downgrade the word of the Lord to a mere personality assessment. Instead of leaping to take unholy stock of another's emotional reactions, we need to learn to recognize genuine spiritual decay.

It would be so easy if there was some kind of gauge we could check to make sure we are in the Lord's will. We can't ever trust our own "thermometer," because we can fail miserably in reading the degree to which we have embraced a lukewarm spirit ourselves. Self-examination will often deceive us into measuring ourselves against others whom we consider "less spiritual," making the Christian walk one of competition and comparison. Yet our spirits stand alone under Heaven's spotlight, and we will be judged individually, not graded on a curve.

Hunger is the primary component in our quest to be "hot" for God. Someone who is "hot" will have a tendency toward perpetual hunger. When I was a young mother, I was told why babies' hunger cries are so persistent and unable to be pacified. They actually experience intense hunger pangs equal to those of an adult going without food for several days. Babies burn up all their fuel every few hours because they are growing so fast — they triple their birth weight in the first year of life. They use up calories and metabolize food much faster than we do. People earnestly seeking God are like that. They are in constant growth, metabolizing what they are fed, and they are always hungry for more.

We must realize, though, that "cold" people can be just as hungry! They just ravenously fill themselves with the wrong kind of "food." They do not receive what the Lord has to offer. Instead, they feed on the world to satisfy their desires. They recognize a void in themselves that needs to be filled, but out of ignorance or rebellion they partake from the wrong plate. The unbeliever who is highly motivated toward a sinful lifestyle often shocks the church when he repents and surrenders his life after an encounter with the Lord. We shouldn't be so surprised! In Luke 7:47, Jesus states that the one who is forgiven much loves much. In other words, that person, more than anyone else, is aware of the true extent of his or her need. After the extreme experience of trying and failing to fill the void in his life, he certainly knows the pain of dissatisfaction and the vastness of the need in his heart. Therefore, when the love of Christ is revealed to him, he recognizes the complete fulfillment that he is being offered.

Both spiritually "hot" and spiritually "cold" people display intensity in their respective conditions. There's no question who they have aligned themselves with. But by definition, *there can be no extremity in being lukewarm.* Complacency is the trademark of a lukewarm

Christian. There is an absence of hunger because there is no recognition of need. A spiritually lukewarm person is like a child who has a pocketful of candy and snacks all day long. He never becomes hungry for a real meal. Hunger is a very good thing. When the body requires food, a weakness comes that alerts us of our need for it. We know that we have to eat regularly or we will die. The lukewarm person is perishing, but doesn't know it. Somehow, he always *feels* full and satisfied with his present condition. Although on some level he may be in church and partake of the things of God, he does not partake of the Lord Himself.

It is the Lord's clever design to keep us dependent on Him. We need Him constantly for His direction and wisdom. We get no report cards to tell us how we're doing. However, He will reveal the impurities in our hearts as we stay in a close relationship and in submission to Him.

If we ask earnestly and listen for His voice, we can expect the Lord to give us discernment about our own lukewarm tendencies. Then we can bring those before the Lord and ask Him to give us supernatural revelation about how we are affected and how He would have us lay them down. Let Him be the Lord of your "thermometer." His assessment is the only one that counts.

CHAPTER 2

A WAKE-UP LETTER

*L*aodicea was the last of the seven churches to receive a personal message from the Lord in the book of Revelation. As is common in the Scriptures, the application of this church's message reaches beyond the original recipient. We should all take this warning to heart.

Every part of the Word of God is eternally fresh. One perspective in the Body of Christ is that the churches in Revelation were not addressed in random order, but rather serve to present a kind of dispensational picture. If that be the case, then we could be living smack in the middle of Laodicea. The Lord may want this generation to soberly acknowledge her sisterhood with this last church that He addressed. If so, it is important to know that if we hold this word up against our own lives and submit to its instruction, we also clearly come in line to inherit the same astounding mercy and blessings that were offered to the Laodiceans.

As Jesus first identifies Himself in Revelation 3:14 as *"the Amen, the Faithful and True Witness, the Beginning of the creation of God,"* we have reason to believe that these people were already keenly aware of the fullness of who He was. In fact, Paul mentions Laodicea in his epistle to the Colossians, and even requests that their letter be read to the Laodicean church. In Colossians 2:1, he expresses the agony he has experienced in praying for both cities (they were only a few miles apart) concerning their susceptibility to false teaching. He later exhorted them:

> *As you therefore have received Christ Jesus the Lord, so walk in Him, rooted and built up in Him and established in the faith, as you have been taught, abounding in it with thanksgiving. Beware lest anyone cheat you through philosophy and empty deceit, according to the tradition of men, according to the basic principles of the world, and not according to Christ.* Colossians 2:6-8

Clearly, the Laodicean church was given some apostolic priority, and their spiritual growth was an ongoing burden for Paul. Colossians was written, scholars say, around A.D. 61. It is believed that Revelation was written sometime between A.D. 64 and A.D. 96, so exactly how much time passed between Paul's admonitions in Colossians and the Lord's rebuke in Revelation is not known. It could have been as few as three years, or as many as thirty-five years. What is apparent is that Paul's early warnings were not heeded, for the Laodicean reprimand by the Lord in Revelation is much harsher than the Colossian account.

In Revelation 3:15-16, the Lord begins His message by immediately addressing the problem:

> *"I know your works, that you are neither cold nor hot. I could wish you were cold or hot. So then, because you are lukewarm, and neither cold nor hot, I will vomit you out of My mouth."*

This was not another pleading appeal to get things right with the Lord, but a graphic and decided rebuke. His utter disgust is definite, but His intent in spitting them out was not just to say, "You make me sick!" They were to be suddenly and forcefully expelled from His presence, possibly in the attempt to make them experience a jolt that would awaken them to their sin. They would be thrust into the stark reality of the separation they had already instigated between themselves and God. They had not been totally forsaken by Him, because He still offered them another chance to make the choice between hot and cold.

Coincidentally, although prosperity abounded and industry thrived in the city of Laodicea, the water supply was limited. Because Laodicea was situated in a valley, the problem had to be remedied by bringing water in through aqueducts that were several miles long. The closest sources of abundant water were the snowcapped mountains above the valley, and hot springs located about five miles from the city. Having access to both very hot and ice cold water would have been an ideal luxury for the day. However, by the time water reached the city through the pipe system, the cold water from the mountains had warmed up and the hot water from the springs had cooled down. It was lukewarm and distasteful to drink. So the Laodiceans were very familiar with the application of the picture Jesus gave them.

The Lord does not detail what will happen when this "spew" takes place. It could be that each one who is guilty of a lukewarm heart has his own kind of expulsion and resulting wilderness to face. Even as the Lord was speaking to the entire church of Laodicea, He was undoubtedly dealing with their souls on an individual basis. In Proverbs 1:32, we see that *the complacency of fools* destroys. In His great mercy, God devised a spiritual thrashing that, if received rightly, would turn the Laodiceans aside from that certain path of destruction.

The Lord always requires His people to commit to faithfully serve Him only. Joshua 24:15 is a prime example:

> *Choose for yourselves this day whom you will serve, whether the gods which your fathers served that were on the other side of the River, or the gods of the Amorites, in whose land you dwell. But as for me and my house, we will serve the LORD."*

God is not going to let us stay in our self-imposed "neutral" zone. Like the children of Israel, whether we are rooted in the traditions of past generations (*"the gods which your fathers served"*), or living in a new city surrounded by "new" gods (*"the gods of the Amorites, in whose land you dwell"*), we have to make a choice to be sold out to the Lord. As all those who claim Christianity, we are either overcoming in our walk with Him, or we are becoming something that will be spit out of His mouth.

I believe one reason the Lord seems so severe about His dealing with the lukewarm church is because His Kingdom has absolutely no purpose for it. A church that is flowing with Him and is engaging in a growing relationship with Him brings Him glory. The people exhibit the fruit and gifts of the Spirit, sowing and reaping in the harvest of the lost. They are His mouth, hands and feet to do the work of the Gospel. As they worship Him fully, His presence manifests in their midst, and He demonstrates His abundant mercy and love.

"Cold" unbelievers also reveal the attributes of God. The condition of their lives advertises the consequences of rejecting the Lord, and the loneliness they project only confirms the desperate need for Him. The punishment of the wicked shows the magnitude of the perfect justice of God, His undeniable power and His kingship. When every knee bows, evil will be forced to acknowledge Jesus as Lord, and that single acknowledgment will settle the eternal conflict once and for all.

However, there is no viable reason for God to endure a lukewarm church in its ongoing state. Claiming to belong to the Lord, these believers depend on flesh to sustain what they will not submit to Him, preventing His glory from ever shining through them. Yet their unwillingness to openly promote immorality makes them an unreliable and inconsistent tool for the enemy. They live in deception that their cause is holy. They become skilled at taking a thread of truth and fabricating a work, which they attribute to the Holy Spirit, yet all the while denying Him access to weave Himself freely into their lives. They say that they have attained to the works of God, but they only champion a worthless trophy engraved with the finest human effort. True ministry can be accomplished only if the Lord is our central passion. We must pursue His purpose and glory alone.

CHAPTER 3

THE SEVEN CHURCHES

*T*he second and third chapters of the book of Revelation contain specific messages from the Lord to seven churches in Asia Minor. The cities were located surprisingly close to each other, especially considering the diversity of their spiritual climates. Their names were: *Ephesus, Smyrna, Pergamos, Thyatira, Sardis, Philadelphia* and *Laodicea*.

Jesus followed a similar pattern in addressing each church. He began by addressing the church by name. He then identified Himself by various attributes of His power and person. The first six churches were greeted with descriptions of things Jesus possesses or has done, such as holding the stars or coming back to life. Laodicea is the only church to which Jesus solely represented His identity by His titles, rather than actions. To the church in Laodicea, He introduced Himself as *"the Amen, the Faithful and True Witness, the Beginning of the creation of God.*" It is significant that, of all the churches, He wanted the Laodiceans to relate to Him personally — not through His works, but for who He was.

After the Lord's salutation, every church received a "works evaluation," along with assorted commands and rebukes. Each message ended with a promise to the overcomers in that city.

The first church, in *Ephesus* (meaning "desirable"), had a favorable report card for good works (see Revelation 2:1-7). Ephesus was praised uniquely for not tolerating evil, wisely testing and exposing false apostles, and not becoming weary in laboring for the Lord. But she had one fault — she had left her *"first love."* She were called to repent and *"do the first works"* or else the Lord would *"come to [her] quickly and remove [her] lampstand from its place."*

The second church, in *Smyrna*, had endured poverty and persecution (see Revelation 2:8-11). The city's name certainly describes the church's tribulation. It means "myrrh," which is a bitter herb often associated with hatred. Jesus encouraged this church for steadfastness in suffering and gave her no rebukes.

The church in *Pergamos* (meaning "fortified" as a tower or castle) was commended for holding fast to the Lord, even as her faith was tested by the martyrdom of one of her own (see Revelation 2:12-17), but some in Pergamos had failed the Lord by embracing the immoral doctrines of false gods. The Lord warned them, *"Repent, or else I will come to you quickly and will fight against them with the sword of My mouth"* (Revelation 2:16).

The fourth church, in *Thyatira*, was approved because her last works were *"more than the first"* (Revelation 2:18:29). She was growing in love and service. However, she was reprimanded for allowing a false prophetess, referred to as Jezebel, to "teach and seduce" in the church. The Lord promised to punish her and those under her influence unless they repented.

To the church in *Sardis*, the Lord's words were sharp (see Revelation 3:1-6). He said, *"I know your works, that you have a name that you are alive, but you are dead"* (Revelation 3:1). This church is called upon to *"strengthen the things which remain"* and repent or *"I will come upon you as a thief."* However, He does exhort some in Sardis whom He says were not defiled.

The sixth church, in *Philadelphia* (meaning "brotherly love"), was honored for her good works by the gift of an open door set before her that could not be shut (see Revelation 3:7-13). She was to be abundantly blessed for her devotion to the Lord. In fact, she received no correction at all. The only other church to escape His reproof was the one in Smyrna, the church that was under severe persecution.

The seventh and final church to be addressed was the one in *Laodicea* (which means "justice/punishment" or "the people rule" [see Revelation 3:14-22]). Jesus did not commend her in any way, and she had no good works. Only Sardis shared this distinction of totally missing the mark in her works. Both of these churches were putting forth a front of deception— Sardis, by perpetuating an "alive" reputation while actually being dead, and Laodicea, by claiming prosperity in the things of God while being spiritually poor. However, the chruch in Laodicea was presented with the strictest requirements for restoration of any of the seven churches.

It is interesting to note that the ones who would heed the Lord's admonitions and eventually become overcomers were given promises that somewhat correlated with the problems of their city. In Ephesus, where believers had lost their taste for the things of God, the overcomers were promised that they would *"eat from the tree of life."* Those in Smyrna, facing martyrdom and death, were promised the *"crown of life."* In the city of Pergamos, where the doctrine of Balaam promoted eating what was sacrificed to idols, the overcomer was promised *"some of the hidden manna to eat."* The church in Thyatira had allowed herself to be ruled by the unrighteous authority of a false prophetess, yet the overcomers could look forward to *"power over the nations."* In Sardis, overcomers would attain life, although their church was dead. An overcoming Philadelphian was to become *"a pillar in the temple."* as reward for being part of a church that diligently stood fast and strong.

There can be no argument that the Lord was gracious in His promises to these churches. His display of mercy, even to the courageous overcomer, is grandly demonstrated. His rewards are lavishly beyond the level deserved, as if any are worthy of a prize for mere obedience to a most holy God. The Laodicean church, more than any of the other churches, should have been considered last in line for the blessings of the Lord.

Her lukewarmness and resulting pride and self-sufficiency undercut any dependence on God, even though she claimed to be His.

Even the church in Sardis, which God considered "*dead,*" was a better place to be in than than the church in Laodicea. She at least had a "name" that she was alive. Apparently, she at least cared about her reputation, and perhaps she even cared about the reflection that was on the Lord. Maybe she was being deceptive by putting up a false façade, but somewhere there had to be a measure of guilt and conviction. Jesus said that there were "a few names" in Sardis who were worthy, and these undoubtedly were a remnant that stood in the gap as a living example. But no shred of righteousness existed in Laodicea.

From the scriptures we are given, Laodicea appears to have been a boastful, arrogant church, where the quality of humility was likely looked upon as spiritual weakness. Flaunting her religious activity before the God to whom she gave little reverence, she provoked Him to vomit her from His mouth. This should have disqualified her from the remotest opportunity for reward.

But, even as the Lord chastises His children, His arms never cease to be open, and His voice never stops pleading for relationship. It bears repeating that the highest promise of reward was given to the overcomers in the Laodicean church. Why? *Because the lukewarm stronghold is the most difficult to overcome.*

When we are confronted with a clear choice of serving Him, it is much easier to stand when that decision brings extreme consequences. In a church like

Smyrna's, beset with tribulation and impending death, there can be no lukewarm decision. One either denies the Lord or makes a total and sacrificial commitment, regardless of possible consequences. When someone wants to be an overcomer in a lukewarm church, however, that person has no momentum to hang onto. He is propositioned by a false peace that renders him free of conflict if he agrees to the conditions, but declares war on him if he doesn't. He is not necessarily tempted with gross sins, but "good things" that will even seem to fill an acceptable quota on his heavenly scorecard. His quandary is not a choice between good and evil, but a temptation to live well, free and easy instead of choosing the best, which will cost him everything. When no one else seems required to lay down his life to thrive, it makes little sense to waste ourselves for a cause that doesn't seem to demand it. This leaves the choice completely up to us.

In exchange for a submitted life, the Lord promised the Laodiceans refined gold (which is faith and purity), white garments (righteousness) and His anointed vision (Revelation 3:18). In exchange for opening the door to the Lord, they would be able to sit face-to-face with Jesus and enjoy great intimacy with Him (Revelation 3:20). And finally, to the overcomer in Laodicea, Jesus promised, *"I will grant to sit with Me on My throne, as I also overcame and sat down with My Father on His throne"* (Revelation 3:21). That is the highest honor the Lord can offer a believer.

The overcomers would conquer a stronghold that

declared that no absolute rule was necessary. They would fight the prevailing belief that they could have led a successful life without groveling homage being paid to any throne, even God's. They would reject every voice in their surroundings that screamed for moderation and lukewarm relief. Truth would become more important than compromising unity, and complete submission to God would become their goal, rather than friendship with the world. The Lord makes it clear that those who had the freedom to choose any degree of spiritual devotion and chose the highest measure possible — even to the demise of their own spiritual comfort — will be the ones who sit closest to Jesus as He rules and reigns.

CHAPTER 4

LOST LOVE

fter evaluating the differences and similarities among the seven churches of Revelation, a conclusion might be drawn that the spiritual problems in Ephesus and Laodicea were much alike. Ephesus was accused of leaving her first love, while Laodicea was reproved for being lukewarm. However, although both of them were accused of indifference toward the Lord, His approach was entirely distinct in each situation.

Abandoning "first love" and being lukewarm are concepts that are often used interchangeably today in the modern church. But there is a marked difference. If they are just two terms for the identical condition, then God is extremely unjust, because He was considerably more harsh with Laodicea than with Ephesus. The difference in approach, therefore, had to be connected to how the two churches had evolved into their respective states.

The Ephesians were admonished to *"Remember therefore from where you have fallen; repent and do the first works"* (Revelation 2:5). It was a simple, three-step plan for recovery — a remembrance of where they had been, a U-turn, and a returning to what they had done before. The consequence for ignoring His call to repentance was the swift removal of their lampstand. As they had cooled in their passion for the Lord, they had begun to run on "old oil," which had not been replenished since they had faltered in their primary focus. Jesus was saying that the anointing they had started to take for granted would not carry them forward anymore, as their hearts had turned aside from their source. Their tenacity and discernment were praised, and they had a full account of good works. But it was as if the Lord was saying, "Hey! Remember Me? You know — the reason you're doing all this? Realize that you are getting sidetracked and get back to the priority of seeking My face."

Note that the first thing God told them to do was *"remember."* In the past, they had been in a love relationship with Him. It had been a honeymoon full of that *"first love."* They apparently had ceased to grow in that direction and had even begun to shrink back. However, they did have a formerly healthy relationship to return to. If they saw the error of their ways, they would be able to resume their intimacy with the Lord.

From all indications, the Laodiceans had no genuine first love to return to. They could not renew a love they never had; theirs had to be created anew.

They had no good works to their credit, and seemingly they had never been in close union with the Lord. For the Lord to ask them to return to a former love would have required them to recall their past point of deepest fervency.

By using their own thermometer, they would have then gauged themselves against their "hottest" memory. But by the Lord's standards, they still would have registered a decided grade of lukewarm. Even though the Laodiceans professed Christ, they had forever kept Him at arm's length.

The Ephesians could be likened to a woman who falls madly in love and gets married. She has a wonderful, fruitful relationship with her husband, and they have several children. However, after years of household responsibility and familiarity, she slowly loses the passion she once felt for her husband.

The Laodiceans had a different kind of relationship with the Lord. They were like a woman who dates a man but refuses to marry him because she has other priorities she wants to pursue. Instead, she engages in an off-and-on, shallow relationship with him, keeping him on a string but never committing to him.

Like the married woman, the Ephesians had experienced an intimate relationship with the Lord that had born, good fruit. The Laodiceans had not even begun. The possibility existed for the Ephesians to be reignited and return to the love of their first commitment, to that "honeymoon" part of the relationship. The Laodiceans had constantly avoided the initial union that would have brought intimacy. The relationship they chose to have with the Lord was one with no capability of bearing fruit. Their only recourse was to submit to the "marriage" — the intimate union — that was proposed in the beginning of the relationship.

The church in Ephesus had known the Lord and His voice. She had reached a maturity in Him where a simple correction was probably all that would be necessary. The Lord was obviously confident of her sensitivity to His voice. His demeanor indicated that He expected her heart to be soft toward Him.

David, who was described as having a heart after God, somehow fell into grievous sin. In 2 Samuel 12, the prophet Nathan came to David and used a parable to expose his sins of adultery and murder. He related God's perspective on what David had done, concluding with the convicting statement, *"You are the man!"* (2 Samuel 12:7). There was no doubt that David was fully aware of the severity of his sins even as he was committing them. One wonders how such a man of God could commit such acts so carelessly. Yet, when the very words of the Lord came to expose those sins, David immediately repented. He knew God, and he knew His voice. He was confronted face-to-face with the Lord through the prophet.

The Ephesians were guilty of "lesser" sins than David was, but only a few years before, Paul had prayed:

> *That Christ may dwell in your hearts through faith; that you, being rooted and grounded in love, may be able to comprehend with all the saints what is*

44

*the width and length and depth and height — to
know the love of Christ which passes knowledge; that
you may be filled with all the fullness of God.*
                                        Ephesians 3:17-19

God was clearly speaking to the Ephesians as a church that had once worshiped Him in the most ardent fashion. Whether they had reached their state of lost love by ignorance or not, they still had a fundamental desire to please the Lord. Ironically, it is probable that the Laodiceans also read the letter from Paul to the Ephesians, as his letters were circulated among the cities in Asia Minor.

Since New Testament times, periodic movements of renewal and revival have helped return lost love to the church. But as the fire of first love can be kindled again by a fresh touch from God, the same results cannot be expected to take place in those born and bred in lukewarmness. They have no point of reference to return to. They have never experienced a true "first love." The staying power of a revival is diminished as this lukewarm flesh is stirred up but never renounced and exchanged for the "real thing." Lukewarm flesh cannot be pushed up a notch to make it acceptable. It might be momentarily propped up to be ecstatic, but in the long run, it cannot maintain pure devotion to the Lord.

Renewal can be defined as "regeneration, resumption, and restoration to fullness." If we are praying for "renewal," how effective can our prayers be? Can the lukewarm *resume* that which they have not yet started?

Can they be *restored* to a condition of love that they have never experienced? A victim of drowning can be revived by breathing air into his lungs. The body can be resuscitated to breathe again by itself. However, a department-store mannequin would never start breathing on its own if it received the same treatment. Those who have lost their first love have forgotten how to "breathe" Jesus into their spirits, but the lukewarm have never really breathed in the first place.

To be genuinely awakened, the lukewarm church must first have a true revelation of the Lord. She needs something beyond renewal or revival. She needs *reformation*. To *reform* is "to change into a new and improved condition; to improve by change of form." It is only as true reformation comes forth in a church that lukewarm strongholds are broken. We need a modern reformation to revolutionize the church as we know it.

The question arises, why didn't the past reformations yield permanent and lasting results? Why are the fortresses of the Laodicean spirit standing even stronger today? In any reformation, human nature dictates that eventually the fervor will fade — especially after the key players move on or pass away. However, the greatest problem arises when people try to pass on the elements of a reformation without the original passion and revelation. The new generation, then, has no understanding of the fire of the original work. As the passion is diluted, those who have no remembrance of the reformation become birthed into a church that has become increasingly void of its initial fire. By the time it gets to them, they accept it "as is." Voids are filled with religious rules and activity, holding the founding fathers up as idols and framing that past move of God with historical awe. Later generations remain ignorant of the inferiority of what they are fed in the name of their dead "grandfathers in the spirit." Without that "first love," they are birthed as lukewarm and know no other way.

It has not only been these past few generations that have struggled to maintain their first love. There are many Old Testament accounts of the strayings of the children of Israel. They had a bad habit of forgetting the Lord, and they had to be constantly nudged back to Him. Devotion eroded and soon gave way to tradition, and the letter of the law became more important than the *Lord* of the law. By the time Jesus came to earth, lukewarm Judaism had become the status quo, and John the Baptist revealed the main downfall of the lukewarm — pride:

> *Do not think to say to yourselves, "We have Abraham as our father." For I say to you that God is able to raise up children to Abraham from these stones. And even now the ax is laid to the root of the trees. Therefore every tree that does not bear good fruit is cut down and thrown into the fire.* Matthew 3:9-10

A few years later, this same sermon could have been preached in Laodicea.

Today, as a whole, our churches have also been birthed into a society that has never been given a revelation of

47

true Christianity. We were born into mediocrity and do not even know it. Therefore, we are quite likely to produce a lukewarm Gospel, complete with factions that will play down the need for personal repentance of sin and a personal decision for Christ. As the Word of God is watered down, it becomes improbable that a true first love will ever be experienced in the first place. When the leadership admonishes the church to return to her first love, she may not have a clue as to what this means. An Ephesian message may, indeed, not be what the church needs to hear. Rather, what she desperately needs is the revelation of her membership in the Laodicean church.

We are in danger of becoming a memorial to the intimacy, power and works of God that He brought to past generations. Some churches are founded by degenerated, "second-generation" leadership and perpetuate that lukewarm quality in those to whom they minister. Some pastors once flowed with God, but are now drying up because of compromise. They are unknowingly teaching a new generation to swim in a dry riverbed with enticing programs and entertainment. They sell their "brand" of church as "normal," fun and even the best that the Lord has to offer. They flaunt their "prosperity" and declare that the anointing of God is on them because of it. However, in the church, "success" cannot necessarily be measured by sphere of influence, media exposure or monetary standards. *The fact that Jesus will accommodate and temporarily concede to the conditions we offer Him does not imply that He has approved of our limitations on Him.*

If past glory becomes a vehicle by which we now do our *works*, we are no longer doing *the* work. Popularity will fuel our ambitions, and our love for the Lord will suffer and become eroded. When we use a slice of truth to our advantage, but are not changed by it ourselves, our religion has every opportunity to become bigger than our God. We have around us in the Western world all the components necessary to assemble a Laodicean monstrosity that will assure us all that we are the cream of the chosen, oblivious to the Lord crying over us like He did over Jerusalem:

How often I wanted to gather your children together, as a hen gathers her chicks under her wings, but you were not willing! Matthew 23:37

CHAPTER 5

FOR SALE — THE BURNING REMEDY

*L*aodicea was a very prosperous city in the first century. It was a center for banking, and was known for producing a rare, glossy black wool that was used in making clothing and carpets. The city had an extensive medical community which was famous for producing an eye salve that was said to cure some eye disorders. Located in a geographic region that was targeted for evangelism, it also had opportunity to share in the wealth of apostolic input that was afforded the early believers. If any church should have been thriving and grateful, it was Laodicea's.

How could the church in such a blessed city become deserving of being spit out of God's mouth? In a word, it was pride. In Revelation 3:17, Jesus begins by saying, *"Because you say, 'I am rich, have become wealthy, and have need of nothing...'."* Yes, she was blessed. She was materially wealthy and had experienced spiritual abundance. Surrounded by this immense fortune, they began to believe she was self-sufficient — perhaps even deserving of all she possessed. In her arrogance, she was totally deceived, unaware of the depravity that had so cleverly overtaken her. Matthew 13:22 says that *"the cares of this world and the deceitfulness of riches choke the word."* The snare of this independence from God had seduced her into a state of ignorant unfruitfulness.

The Laodiceans were totally unaware that they were *"**wretched**, miserable, poor, blind, and naked"* (Revelation 3:17). In contrast, in Romans 7:24, we find the Apostle Paul grieving over his carnal nature, which was constantly at war against his desire to be controlled by the Lord. He laments, *"O **wretched** man that I am! Who will deliver me from this body of death?"* The same Greek word is used for *"wretched"* in of both these passages — *talaiporos* — which means "contemptible, despicable, and worthless." Paul knew that his own heart was full of the capacity for sin, and he acknowledged that the Lord was his only hope for the salvation and deliverance of his flesh.

If we do not know that we, too, are wretched, then our carnal nature will not be offensive to us. In fact, it may seem quite acceptable. We live according to what pleases us at the time, and not by the Word of God. The greater our desire is to live in His presence, the greater the realization of our own inability to live there in our present state. When we admit our wretchedness, we are not suffering from incredibly low self-esteem, but we are clearly aware of our unrighteousness in the light of the holiness of God. Seeing this, our own flesh becomes detestable to us, and we see its worthlessness.

Somehow, the Laodiceans had also escaped know-ing that they were indeed *miserable* (Greek, *eleeinos*). This word denotes the kind of misery that others should respond to by showing great pity because so much hardship has been endured. Paul uses that same Greek word in 1 Corinthians 15:19: *"If in this life only we have hope in Christ, we are of all men the most **pitiable**."*

Probably the most difficult accusation for the Laodiceans to accept was that they were *"poor."* They lived in a city with great material wealth, yet in the Kingdom of God, they were beggars. They were not living in the abundance that the Lord had to offer them as His children. Matthew 6:21 says, *"For where your trea-sure is, there your heart will be also."* They had put their confidence in earthly wealth instead of in the riches of the Lord, and their hearts were far from Him.

The Laodiceans were oblivious to their spiritual con-dition, and they had certainly proven themselves to be *"blind."* They were "home blind." That is, they had a self-assessed sight that did not allow them to see the truth.

Finally, God reveals that the Laodicean church was "naked." Again, their natural environment played a prophetic role in pointing out their spiritual condition. Laodicea produced an exotic black wool used in mak-ing clothing — a wool so rare that it is no longer even produced. Yet, spiritually, the Laodiceans did not have any shame, and were not clothed in His righteousness. When Adam and Eve sinned, they realized their na-kedness and hid from the Lord. The Laodiceans were so calloused that they had no sensitivity to their own sin or "nakedness" before God.

In John 15:22, Jesus says, *"If I had not come and spoken to them, they would have no sin, but now they have no excuse for their sin."* Even though the Lord did say that the Laodiceans refused to see their wretchedness, they could not claim an innocent ignorance. He had tried to intervene in their lives, but they had continually rejected Him.

He had sent His word to them through the epistles of Paul, but they did not heed His concerns for them. They had adopted an *"I have no need of you"* philosophy toward the Lord and His Body, ignoring His attempts to both build them up and help them avoid the pitfalls that they eventually fell into.

What are the consequences if we refuse to acknowledge our unrighteousness before our holy God? In Isaiah 6, the prophet Isaiah, who was privileged to exclaim, *"I saw the Lord,"* responded to the experience by saying, *"Woe is me, for I am undone!* [meaning "brought to silence," or even "destroyed"] *because I am a man of unclean lips."* It was with this acknowledgment of his own filth that the Lord sent one of the seraphim with a live coal to touch his lips and cleanse him from his sin. As a result, Isaiah was able to confidently answer the call from God, *"Here am I! Send me."* If Isaiah, who was a faithful servant and prophet of God, experienced such agony at the confrontation of his own sin, what are the consequences for those of us who would presume to come into His presence in the pride of our own wealth and in *"need of nothing*"? We will surely be brought to our knees, but the pain will be devastating because we have such a long way to fall.

The ongoing awareness of our sinful nature is the catalyst that insures the purging process will continue in our lives. Our relationship with the Lord depends on it. We will not shrink back if we remain mindful that one day we will see the Lord face-to-face.

In His grace, the Lord even has a remedy for outright, willful defiance. What He offers is not always easy medicine to swallow, but it always brings full recovery and healing. The church in Laodicea was terminally ill with a "lukewarm virus," and the prescription was found in the words of Jesus in Revelation 3:18.

In Revelation 3:18, Jesus says, *"I counsel you to buy from Me gold refined in the fire."* Incredibly, the Lord did not command, but only *counseled* them to follow His direction. This word, *counsel*, is not a particularly strong word; it merely means "recommend." In the middle of this scorching rebuke, the almighty God simply gives His "recommendation." He cared for them immensely, but they had made the decision to be lukewarm, and it could only be reversed by another choice of free will. The Laodiceans had to approach the Lord deliberately and humbly with a desire to drastically change.

The first stipulation for the "cure" was to *"buy from Me gold refined in the fire, that you may be rich."* (Revelation 3:18). They were required to buy something from God Himself! How were they to buy from the Lord, and how much would it cost?

When we want to buy something, we must first of all declare that we have a need for something that we do not have. Then we must look for a willing seller who has what we want. The Laodiceans had to become buyers who would humble themselves before the great Seller and petition Him, saying, "There is something we do not have, but You do; we need to receive this from You." Recognition of need was an important first step for this self-sufficient church.

When we approach the Seller, we do it realizing that in the course of the transaction, our worth will decrease while His increases. The cost of the item we are purchasing determines how much our worth decreases to obtain it. God's prices are astronomically high. He will not take money or worldly goods in exchange. He requires the life of the buyer. He says, *"Present your bodies a living sacrifice, holy, acceptable to God, which is your reasonable service"* (Romans 12:1-2). That is the only payment that He will accept.

In Luke 14:28, Jesus says, *"For which of you, intending to build a tower, does not sit down first and count the cost, whether he has enough to finish it?"* When we count the cost, we then can decide if we want to pursue an exchange with the Seller.

We must also realize that God is the only one who "sells" what we really need. Matthew 25 tells the parable of the ten virgins who took their lamps with them to meet the bridegroom. Five brought extra oil for their lamps, and five did not. When their lamps ran low, the foolish virgins asked for oil from the wise ones who had brought extra. The wise virgins refused them, saying, *"Go rather to those who sell, and buy for your-selves."* We, too, must go to the "seller" of the oil, and the Spirit of God is the only source.

If we are willing for our worth to decrease to obtain all God has for us, we will not do it halfheartedly. We will give ourselves without hesitating, knowing that *"the kingdom of heaven is like treasure hidden in a field, which a man found and hid; and for joy over it he goes and sells all that he has and buys that field."* (Matthew 13:44). John the Baptist expressed that he considered himself privileged that his worth was decreasing to usher in the increasing ministry of Jesus: *"The friend of the bridegroom, who stands and hears him, rejoices greatly because of the bridegroom's voice. Therefore, this joy of mine is fulfilled. He must increase, but I must de-crease"* (John 3:29-30).

The centurion whose servant was ill did not even consider himself worthy enough that Jesus should enter his house (see Luke 7:6-9). Jesus marveled at the man's faith because he knew it was not necessary for Jesus to physically be on the premises to perform a miracle. Why did this man have such great faith? As a soldier, the centurion understood how authority op-erated, and therefore, he knew that what Jesus com-manded would be done. His humility demonstrated that he had a revelation of his own sinful nature. In light of his realization of unworthiness, he also real-ized that God's power was unlimited. The result was a concrete belief that Jesus could do anything. Like the centurion, as we are emptied of our own worth, we are then open to be filled with the knowledge of

His worth. That is the point at which we will give all to buy what He has.

In buying from the Lord, there is one requirement that is not open for negotiation: We must take up His cross. In Mark 10:22, the rich ruler left Jesus in great sorrow, because he was not willing to sell all he had and take up the cross. As Matthew 10:38 says, *"He who does not take his cross and follow after Me is not worthy of Me."* This demonstrates that we can disqualify ourselves on this one point from being worthy buyers.

We must follow the example of Jesus, who was *"crucified in weakness"* (2 Corinthians 13:4). We must nail all our strength to the cross until our flesh becomes weak and dies. Our goal should be to be able to say, *"I have been crucified with Christ; it is no longer I who live, but Christ lives in me."* (Galatians 2:20). Even though the Lord addressed the church of Laodicea as a whole, the decision to offer oneself completely to Him and take up the cross was and will always be a personal decision.

Many years ago, the Lord touched my life deeply during a church service. As most of the congregation was crowded at the altar, I cried as I felt a new consecration and surrender coming in my relationship with Him. As the service ended and people began to leave, I found that I could not stop my tears, and turned to my husband, hoping he would comfort me. As he put his arms around me, it was as if I had on a heavy coat. I couldn't even feel his embrace, and I was not comforted in the least. As I walked back down the aisle to leave the sanctuary, I questioned why this had happened during this fresh abandon. The Lord interrupted my thoughts and spoke to me in a very strong and clear voice. He said, *"When you die, you die alone."* You see, every Laodicean who heard the word of the Lord also had to make his own choice for surrender. Each one had to carry his own cross and "die alone."

When we feel smothered by a lukewarm church situation, we have a decision to make. We cannot blame the leadership for our own lack of passion for the Lord, even if every force of hell is working through them to discourage us and kill our fervency.

Once we have made the choice to follow Jesus completely, we have agreed to carry the cross and we cannot separate ourselves from the death that goes along with it. The decision to become a "buyer" comes with the realization that our whole life and worth will be placed on the altar.

As we totally surrender to the Lord, what we have "bought" from Him comes forth. What is placed on the altar is always consumed in some fashion. The gold we "buy" is "refined in the fire." It is a fire of testing:

> *You have been grieved by various trials, that the genuineness of your faith, being more precious than gold that perishes, though it is tested by fire, may be found to praise, honor, and glory at the revelation of Jesus Christ.* 1 Peter 1:6-7

The Laodiceans suffered from a profound lack of genuine faith, choosing instead to put their hope in riches and in their own abilities. The Lord was essentially saying, "If you will lay everything you hold dear on the altar — your pride, abilities, trust in riches, the right to choose your own way — then I will consume all that is not of Me, and what will emerge is a pure and holy faith. Then you will really be rich."

The Lord offered something beyond salvation to Laodicea. As we are saved through faith in the redemptive work of Christ, there is no other work to be done to achieve salvation. Yet, on top of that, what the Lord offered and still offers is the opportunity for maturity and a close relationship with Him.

> *For He is like a refiner's fire and like a launderers' soap. He will sit as a refiner and a purifier of silver; He will purify the sons of Levi, and purge them as gold and silver, that they may offer to the LORD an offering in righteousness.* Malachi 3:2-3

In the Old Testament, the tribe of Levi was set apart to be the priests of the Lord, and they were called to a higher level of consecration. However, they also had the privilege of ministering to the Lord and coming closest to His presence. Their higher call brought greater responsibility and accountability. As servants of Jesus Christ, we will not despise the work of refinement God wants to bring when we realize that it prepares us to fulfill our highest purpose in His Kingdom.

When I was in high school, I began to have an increased desire to live for the Lord. I was extremely blessed to be singled out to be discipled by my youth leaders, and I had many opportunities to be taught the Word of God and to fellowship with believers my own age. At the same time, however, I became keenly aware that I had it easy. I had everything I needed: I was popular and was involved in prestigious school activities. It started to bother me because somehow, even in my immaturity, I knew that I would never become a woman of faith without something to refine me. I did not have a crucified life by any means. I was worldly, weak and undisciplined.

So, in a moment of youthful zeal, I did something I would not recommend for anyone to do lightly. Knowing I needed a greater dependence on Him and desperation for Him, I prayed for the Lord to send trials into my life. I am not advocating what I did as a naïve, awkward teenager, but surrendering ourselves to brokenness to build a deeper faith in Him does please the Lord. I know only too well from firsthand experience that He *will* answer that kind of prayer.

Besides gold refined in the fire, the Laodiceans were also instructed to purchase *"white garments, that [they] may be clothed, that the shame of [their] nakedness may not be revealed"* (Revelation 3:18). The work of God would not be complete in us if He simply stripped us of everything that is not of Him. The Lord does not leave us empty and uncovered; rather, He clothes us in His righteousness. His intent is not to bring shame, but conviction that sends us running to be sheltered under His care. White garments are what people wear in Heaven.

They are a reminder that we have access to the throne of God and that the Lord remembers our sin no more.

The harsh judgments that were brought against the Laodiceans were tempered by God's abundant mercy. We are to "buy" the white garments, but the Lord is the one who puts them on us. When Adam and Eve sinned, in their shame, they sewed fig leaves together to hide their nakedness from the Lord. But after God pronounced the consequences of their sin, Genesis 3:21 says, *"Also for Adam and his wife the Lord God made tunics of skin, and clothed them."* It doesn't say that the Lord created that skin — it would have had to come from an animal He Himself killed. It was the first picture of blood sacrifice — and a reference to Jesus as our slain sacrifice. The Lord made the tunics, and He Himself clothed Adam and Eve.

We cannot clothe ourselves with fig leaves, because in God's eyes, we will still be uncovered. The Laodiceans had sewn fig leaves out of their own brand of wealth and works, not knowing that their covering was unacceptable to God. They had no shame. But the covering they needed came from Jesus—from His sacrifice and the shedding of His blood. In Revelation 7:14, the saints' robes are *"made white in the blood of the Lamb."* Both our righteousness and the remedy for our shame rest in the work of the cross.

Chapter 6

Open Your Eyes
and Answer His Voice

The next counsel the Lord gave to the church of the Laodiceans was, *"Anoint your eyes with eye salve, that you may see"* (Revelation 3:18). Unlike the gold, this was not something to be "bought" from the Lord. It was a directive they were to follow. God had already declared them blind, and He proceeded to show them how that blindness might be healed.

This is the only mention of eye salve in the Bible, and it is speaking of a poultice. A poultice is a soft, paste-like substance that is heated and applied to a wound.

In yet another "prophetic coincidence," Laodicea was famous for producing a medicine that was an effective treatment for various eye ailments. Through

His statement to the church of the Laodiceans, the Lord was making an obvious analogy between natural eye disease and their spiritual blindness.

God did not mention how they were to obtain this special eye salve that was to anoint their eyes. He did not tell them how to get this anointing substance, because they already had it in their possession. They were as familiar with His anointing as they were with the eye salve that was common in their city. His anointing had already been deposited in their spirits and upon their hands — they just weren't using it. The Lord did not say, "Let *Me* anoint your eyes." He said *"You* do it. Take the anointing I've already given you and apply it." If they applied the anointing to their lives, they would be able to clearly behold the Lord and His purposes.

Jesus used dirt mixed with His own spittle to make the clay that He rubbed on the eyes of a blind man. As the man went and washed his eyes in water, he was healed. Jesus was reinforcing the statement He had made shortly prior to this, *"I am the light of the world. He who follows Me shall not walk in darkness, but have the light of life"* (John 8:12). As our spiritual eyes are anointed, the light of Jesus comes rushing into our darkness as well.

When this man was healed, he did not immediately recognize Jesus as the Son of God because he had never seen Him before. But the Lord said to him, *"You have both seen Him and it is He who is talking with you"* (John 9:37). The man immediately responded by both believing and worshiping Jesus.

The anointing does something amazing to us when our eyes are opened and we recognize Jesus for who He is. We have the revelation we need to enter into right relationship with Him. We receive the vision we need to do what God wants us to do. Jesus said that to see Him was to see the Father. He could say that because of their complete oneness, not just because He was an "official" part of the Godhead: He *saw* what the Father was doing and He flowed with it (see John 5:19). In Acts 2, when the Holy Spirit fell, how did they know what to do? The Lord had told them to wait in Jerusalem for the enduement of power, but they were not told exactly what to expect. But when the anointing fell, their spiritual eyes were opened, and they had perfect vision of what to do.

I have heard it said that when Kathryn Kuhlman ministered, at times she would point into the vast audience and declare with all honesty, "*He's* more real to me than *you* are!" If we apply that anointing that gives us perfect vision, we will have the ability to see past thousands of people and every earthly distraction, to gaze straight into the face of the Lord. The reason that this doesn't usually happen for us is because we fail to apply the anointing that has already been given us. If we would be willing to walk in the light that we already have, we would find that an endless supply of revelation would begin to invade our lives.

The anointing, the power or essence of God, is the oil of the Holy Spirit. We cannot claim to be anointed and at the same time resist the Holy Spirit. The kind of relationship *we* choose to have with Him will determine what happens in our everyday lives. It isn't about going to a service where someone is "anointed" and willingly submitting to receiving something through them. The Holy

Spirit is the one who gives us understanding of the Scriptures (see 1 John 2:27), He is the oil of joy, and the joy of the Lord is our strength (see Nehemiah 8:10). After Jesus ascended into Heaven, the Holy Spirit came that we might do the supernatural works of God. If we are only seeking a measure of the Spirit through someone else or through a ministry, then we are missing the fullness of the Spirit.

Likewise, Revelation 3:20 tells us that we, like the Laodiceans, must not only "see" the Lord and sense where and how He is moving, but we must also be able to *hear* His voice for ourselves. We can't always wait for someone else to tell us what He is saying.

I once met a young woman who shared her testimony with me. She had been considering a relationship with the Lord, but she was unsure of the reality of Jesus and whether she should become a Christian. She had tried to read the Bible, but she was still unsure of her rightful access to God. She finally said, "Lord, if I need to be saved, show me." With that, she randomly flipped her Bible open. Her eyes fell on the verse, *"Behold, I stand at the door and knock. If anyone hears My voice and opens the door, I will come in to him and dine with him, and he with Me"* (Revelation 3:20). She was overwhelmed that Jesus was offering her a personal relationship with Him, and received Him that very minute.

No one could doubt that the scripture was a two-edged sword that both cut away her doubt and softened her heart to receive the Lord. I'm sure that at the time she had little idea how many evangelistic messages have contained that very passage as an invitation to countless others. After all, it is the Word of God and does not return void (see Isaiah 55:11). The wooing of Jesus is irresistible to anyone who is open to it.

However, fitting into its context, this verse reveals more about the Lord than His simple request to enter our lives. This verse, in my opinion, is tragic. How devastating it is to realize that this was not written as a call to the lost, but to the Lord's own people! Imagine His heartache, standing outside of a life He had already redeemed, waiting for the entrance He had been promised.

As the Laodicean believers were oblivious to their wretched and miserable spiritual condition, they were also quite unaware that there was a door between them and the Lord. Their relationship with Him had been so superficial that they did not even notice that He was not in the same room with them. That being the case, how long, then, had He been standing outside, knocking on the door? The phrasing used in this scripture suggests an abiding and continuing that implies "covenant." In other words, He had never left, but continued to stand there, patiently waiting. At this very moment, His face is pressed against the door of our resistance and hardness of heart. Everything in us that rejects Him becomes part of that door.

Jesus says, *"Behold, I stand at the door and knock. If anyone hears My voice and opens the door, I will come in to him"* (Revelation 3:20). Notice that He doesn't say, "If you hear Me *knocking*, let me in," but rather, "If you hear My *voice* ... ." The scripture asks for a response to the *voice* of God. Consider that it is His *voice* that is knocking on our hearts, not His knuckles. Jeremiah 23:29 says the word of the Lord is *"like a hammer that breaks the rock in pieces."* His words are coming to penetrate our hearts so that we will let Him in.

In Song of Solomon 5:2, contains a strikingly similar incident: *"I sleep, but my heart is awake; it is the voice of my beloved! He knocks, saying, 'Open for me, my sister, my love, my dove, my perfect one; for my head is covered with dew, my locks with the drops of the night.'"* Observe that in this passage, too, it is His *voice* that the Shulamite hears and responds to, not a rap on the door. And what is her response? She says it is too much trouble to get out of bed and put on her robe to come to the door. Are we so complacent and consumed with our own agendas that we will lock the Lord out of our lives too?

Will the "Laodicean" church hear the Lord knocking at her door today? How can we hear Him when we may not even have the discernment to realize that we have slammed the door in His face? For those in a position to minister, you should be speaking into your churches what the Lord is saying in His knocking. You are doorkeepers in the House of the Lord, and if the ministers are not hearing His voice, then Jesus may not have the means to manifest His voice clearly to a congregation. His knocking will simply go unnoticed or ignored. Jeremiah 7:34 states that when the voice of the bridegroom ceases, the land will become desolate. If the Lord is kept outside of our churches, then most assuredly His voice will not be heard inside, and our brothers and sisters in the Lord will also be left desolate.

CHAPTER 7

ZEAL TO RUN

*T*he Laodiceans received a more rigorous rebuke than any of the other churches in Revelation. Tempered with knowledge of and compassion for their weakness, the Lord reminded them of His consistent care for them. Surely, He understood that they might also fight discouragement after such a chastisement.

Jesus assured them, *"As many as I love, I rebuke and chasten."* This was consistent with Proverbs 3:12, which says, *"For whom the Lord loves He corrects, just as a father the son in whom he delights."* It is interesting that the Laodicean church was the only one of the seven churches that was told the Lord loved her, even though she had rejected His love possibly more than any of them. What an outpouring of mercy! Those who have failed Him the most are frequently the least confident that His forgiveness and love are still available to them.

The kind of love the Lord declares having for the Laodiceans is the Greek word *phileo*. It refers to friendship that includes a sense of sentimental feeling as well as commitment. As the Lord opens His arms of acceptance, He exhorts them to *"therefore be zealous and repent"* (Revelation 3:19). Zeal would have definitely not been an ingrained characteristic of a lukewarm Laodicean. Yet the Lord was not asking for just any kind of repentance, but the enthusiastic kind, which would go against their very nature. God was looking, not just for the fruit of their repentance, but fruit *in* their repentance. Being zealous about their repentance would prove their intent to ardently pursue Him.

True contrition of heart will renounce the lukewarm spirit and eagerly take hold of a burning desire to please the Lord. It comes with an overwhelming conviction of our need to conform to His image. Zeal in repentance will infiltrate every area of our lives.

To be zealous for His power, presence or gifts is pleasing to the Lord. It shows that we want to know His fullness in our lives. However, it also means that we may want God to give us something good that will bless us. That isn't necessarily bad or selfish; God is generous and loves to bless us. However, we should seek to have that same kind of zeal in repentance. Just as much as we have a zeal to be filled up by Him, we should have a zeal to be purged by Him, knowing that He will draw us nearer to Him.

To repent from lukewarmness is to renounce it and begin to think and behave in a new way. The decision to turn from it is ours, but the power to live out our decision can only come from the Holy Spirit. The benefits we derive from our own repentance will be increased only if we will allow God to continue to break all callousness from us. It is not a onetime breaking; rather, it is an ongoing brokenness that we need. Only then can we begin to experience the tenderness that will bring restoration and future sensitivity to the Spirit of God.

The fact that one caught in a lukewarm state would not know his own dilemma and could only be made aware of it by the Lord's verbal intervention should cause us to reevaluate how we view our own sin. Our self-vision is not reliable. If we were *really* zealous, we would not wait for the Lord to interrupt our lives with unexpected reproof. Wisdom should urge us to open our spirits and earnestly ask the Lord to openly reveal our impurities, which we inevitably must face anyway.

There is always room for zeal when we focus on the kind of love that would die on a cross to redeem us. But in our day-to-day lives, drumming up zeal without a momentary reason often stumps us. Song of Solomon 1:4 says, *"Draw me away! We will run after you."* This verse is sung in several beautiful worship songs, but I wonder what we are really thinking when we sing it to the Lord. Each of us has a different expectation of the Lord when we sing "draw me" and a different way we promise to "run" after Him — usually *after* He shows up. The intent of this passage was not supposed to mean, "Okay, Lord, You do *this*, and then I will do *that*." We heartily agree to run after the Lord with zeal *just as soon* as He does something special for us. One person's "draw me; *then* I'll run after You" might really mean, "Heal me, or turn this situation around; *then* I'll really be able to love You and believe in You." Maybe we aren't *that* demanding. Perhaps we only put "little" stipulations on the Lord—no big deal, we just need a little push to get going. "Draw me and I'll run after You" just means, "Let the anointing fall, pour out a bucket of Your presence, *then* I'll feel like worshiping You during this service."

We may not literally say these things, but many times we limit our expressions of devotion to the Lord to mere knee-jerk responses. Isn't He worthy of more than that? We sometimes put heavy requirements on the One we love, even though we don't even deserve what He has already done for us. What if we changed our "draw me" prayers? What if we became vulnerable and asked the Lord to pour a fresh zeal into our "draw me's" and even more passion into our "I'll run's"? What if our eyes were opened to how He wants us to see Him? What if He really became our chief Lover-Bridegroom, who has already proven His love for us by paying the ultimate sacrifice? What if our "draw me and I'll run after you" meant, "Jesus, just crook Your little finger and I'll obey You. I'll do anything," or, "Just whisper my name, and I'll be on my knees immediately, giving You my undivided attention." Wouldn't He be pleased? Yes, that sounds like a zealous prayer.

Let me challenge you to take that a step further. Realize that the Lord is *continually* drawing you. Yes, He is! It is not a special invitation for special occasions; He is always calling His bride to come to Him. Most of the time, we just miss it. Both the eternal and the momentary reason for your zeal is always, *always* before you.

Sometimes we expect Him to dangle a spiritual token to let us know He's beckoning us. But often, the Lord's method of "drawing" us is the opposite of what we expect. He sometimes *withdraws* His manifest presence to get our attention instead of giving us the *wooing* we often wait for. We think He has backed off, so we do too! Somehow, we think it is okay to withhold from Him if we believe He is withholding from us. But God never leaves us or forsakes us (see Hebrews 13:5). All He is doing is drawing you to chase Him — not for His benefit, but to stir up your longing and determination toward Him. That being the case, doesn't it make sense that if God is *always* drawing us, shouldn't we *always* be running? We should never stop! Even then, we will never catch up!

True zeal is proactive, not passive. We can have a form of zeal that is passive; we can respond to the Lord with everything in us, but always wait for Him to make the first overture. What if we didn't wait and, instead, started making advances toward *Him*? James 4:8 even says, *"Draw near to God and He will draw near to you."* Worship Him *before* you feel Him drawing you to it. Tell Him you love Him *before* some great anointing hits you. But I warn you, God will not be outdone, and He will not let you get away with it for long. He will sneak up when you're not paying attention, and you'll suddenly realize that His presence is there. He'll say, "I love you! Gotcha first!" It's like trying to outgive God; you'll never be able to do it, but go ahead and try anyway. Give Him your all!

If you are already running after Him, the drawing will not go away. No, it will only intensify, because God will not have to turn cartwheels to get your attention. You will become so sensitized to His Spirit that His slightest movement will leave you breathless. You will be overwhelmed by His voice when others around you barely notice He is there. Our goal should be to attain an unending, unquenchable zeal for God. So let our highest desire be this prayer:

Jesus, I want to live my life in the cloud of revelation of knowing You are always drawing me. You always desire my worship and fellowship. You're always waiting for me to come to You with open arms. I want my heart to be convinced of it. Deliver me from putting requirements on You or on my feelings before I will come to You. You have already proven Yourself to me. You have already drawn me to Your heart.

I want to live my life in a dead run after You. I never want to stop running after You. I don't want to pause and wait because I need to hear it from You again. If it were possible, You would never have to draw me again because I would already be there, right where You want me — right at Your feet, seeking Your face.

Chapter 8

The Goldilocks Dilemma

An interesting analogy came to me about the choices we make in the Kingdom of God. The children's story "Goldilocks and the Three Bears" is the backdrop for this parable.

Goldilocks represents the lukewarm Christian. She is not content to stay under the obedience and protection of her Father and His house. She is always wandering around outside, although she usually never strays too far off. One day, she stumbles upon a little dirt path and decides to follow it. She doesn't seem to notice the signpost that reads, "The Road of Presumption."

As she travels, Goldilocks comes upon an inviting cottage. Although she is not criminal by nature, her curiosity and emotions drive her inside. She enjoys the freedom of following her own whims. She secretly wishes that she could have her very own little house of comfort like this one, where she could choose her own life instead of living the life her Father has planned for her.

As she enters the house, she comes upon three bowls. The first one is very big, and is full of steaming, hot porridge. She passes by it quickly, feeling a twinge of guilt. It is just the kind of meal they serve at her Father's table, and is the very thing she would like to forget. "That would be way too hot!" she reasons. "I'm not hungry enough to eat all that anyway!" *What she rejects is the kind of spiritual food that the Lord wants to offer us — fresh, hot and in great abundance.*

She notices a second bowl, but, strangely, it's not steaming at all, so she puts her finger in to take a taste. It is stone cold; in fact, a cold so foreign to her that she jumps back in fright. She wonders if it is even porridge, and if it might be poisonous. *This is the kind of satisfaction the enemy offers — it seems to be almost as filling as what God offers, and it is an easier serving for some to eat. Many will not touch it, though, because the taste is too unfamiliar. Some of the enemy's "food" — the teachings of cults and of the world — are so blatantly opposed to basic Judeo-Christian values that they even frighten away those who only have a shallow grounding in the Lord.*

But just then, her fears are calmed as she sees a third bowl. It's so cute and is the perfect size for her small appetite. It's just enough for a quick snack. She cautiously tastes it, and is delighted to find that it is neither hot nor cold, but just right! *This is the attraction of lukewarm teaching. One is not required to fill up on too much of God's Word, and what is given is toned down to a "pleasing temperature." It is adapted to make it socially acceptable. The assumption is that the bride of Christ is a finicky little girl who must be appeased or she will not eat.* And so, with the porridge to her liking, she eats it all.

Next, Goldilocks decides to go exploring through the house. She soon comes to three chairs. The first one is huge and ornate. Her Father has one like it at home. She always thought His chair was too austere and hard, and it looked very uncomfortable. She hastens to walk away. *The chairs represent power and authority. The church that shrinks back from the true authority of God will look upon it as hard — difficult to enforce, unyielding and intolerant. His throne speaks of ultimate justice, and many prefer Him only in His mercy.*

The second chair is smaller, but looks much too soft. Goldilocks imagines herself sitting there, sinking all the way down into it, as though it was quicksand. She is wary of how she could ever sit up straight in it, and she wonders how she could get out of it when she wanted to. *The seat of the enemy looks comfortable at first, but even common sense will tell you that his authority is on shaky ground. Although complacent Christians may not dare to operate in the power of God, they are perhaps even more hesitant to operate in the power of Satan. For the lukewarm, ANY kind of supernatural power is often rejected. Heaven may seem too hard, but hell is too scary!*

Predictably, Goldilocks comes upon the third chair. She's delighted; it's the prettiest little chair she has ever seen. It's small enough not to appear threatening. As she sits down to try it out, immediately the chair breaks and she falls flat on the floor. Feeling foolish, she moves quickly to the next room. *Goldilocks Christians want to keep both feet on the floor while they take on whatever authority makes them feel comfortable. However, that concept falls apart, because we cannot piecemeal a false authority in the flesh. It cannot stand. As Jesus says in Matthew 12:30, "He who is not with Me is against Me." There are only two seats of power — light and darkness. Even the devil exercises authority, however unrighteous, within his own realm. But there is no seat of authority on the lukewarm fence.*

Finally, Goldilocks finds the bedroom. She approaches the first bed. As usual, she encounters something too big and encompassing for her taste, and her Father comes to mind. She is so tired that she doesn't even want to exert the energy to climb onto such a big bed. Besides, it doesn't look that comfortable anyway. *Beds represent two things — rest and intimacy. Lukewarm Christians are unwilling to be completely intimate with the Lord and enter His rest.*

The second bed reminds her of the soft chair. Obviously, they belong to the same person. Even though the size is not as intimidating as that of the first bed, the mattress looks like it wouldn't support her. She doesn't trust that bed at all. *Open promises of happiness and peace from the enemy are suspicious. He is very clever about breaking down defense mechanisms, but those whose spiritual passion is dormant usually shun intimate spiritual encounters of any kind.*

Suddenly, her eyes catch a glimpse of the sweetest little bed she has ever seen. It looks so comfortable and warm. There are lots of pillows and even stuffed animals to keep her company. It looks so inviting that

Goldilocks decides to take a nap. *The "rest" of the luke-warm lifestyle can look very inviting. Children's beds to-day are designed to coerce them to dreamland and soothe bedtime hesitancy. Some are even shaped like cars or dollhouses to make them seem like toys. They are outfitted with fluffy, bright comforters with familiar characters, dispelling the fear of being in a dark and lonely room. The lukewarm influence does the same thing to God's children. It promises peaceful rest, surrounding them with amusements and covering them with "comforters" that are not THE Comforter. Gimmicks promoting a "fun" relationship with God invite them to hide their fears in fantasy.*

Feeling quite secure and cozy, Goldilocks goes to sleep. The next thing she knows, she is awakened by a presence in the room. There are three bears! She is awestruck by the biggest one, and the next biggest is terrifying enough. Thankfully, the baby bear doesn't look dangerous. She is relieved, since there may be a matter to settle of an empty bowl and a broken chair! But, much to her surprise, the little cub points straight at her and says, "There she is!" Shocked to her senses, Goldilocks jumps up and runs home as fast as she can.

Many in the church are sound asleep in their lukewarmness, but the time is coming when they will be confronted for their illegal entry into the house of comfort. God's children should not entertain thoughts of following any course other than staying absolutely committed to Him. When we avoid full allegiance to Him to pursue the presumptuous path of options, we have left His guidance and protection. Many times, our wanderings are not that deliberate. We simply try to see how long we can dance on the fringes of the outer court rather than seek the Lord's face with all our hearts.

When Goldilocks is confronted with the consequences of her wanderings, the biggest bear is not the one who will make the accusation. Those who represent the Father and the true Church will never condemn the ones who need to repent and come home. They will pray for them, challenge and minister to them.

The next biggest bear will not point a finger at the church either. But, why not? After all, Satan *is* the accuser of the brethren. But as long as the lukewarm stay in a temperate zone that is detestable to God, the enemy is pleased and will not chase them from their comfortable state.

When someone in the sleeping church starts to wake up, those who facilitate the practice of lukewarm Christianity will be the first to judge. That lukewarm, cuddly little bear secretly fears his own exposure and will become fierce in order to protect his territory.

The only way Goldilocks can escape is to run home to the Father. Like the prodigal son, we must stop coveting the rewards of our inheritance and spending it unwisely out of the presence of the One who gave it to us. The prodigal son came back humbly, willing to be a servant in the house where he was once an heir. The lukewarm church must surrender herself to and find her comfort in the Father alone. Only then can she be restored and perfected.

CHAPTER 9

CAUGHT IN THE BALANCE

I once attended a church meeting where the seasoned pastor, who had been in ministry for fifteen years, shared his heart with prospective members. He began by relating an event that, he claimed, had given him meaningful direction about his church.

One morning, he was scheduled for back-to-back appointments with two different members of his congregation. The first one came in and said, "Pastor, I enjoy praise and worship in our church. But it seems like we just get started, then we stop. We sing only a few choruses, and there's not really a breakthrough. We don't linger in the presence of God long enough to allow Him to move in a greater way." As the pastor listened, he thought, "He might be right. Maybe we need to give more time to worship."

As the man left, the pastor's next appointment came in and immediately stated the reason for his visit. He said, "Pastor, I come to services here every Sunday. But I have a problem. We just spend too much time singing. I mean, my back starts to hurt and I just can't stand up that long. I also wish we would sing more traditional hymns. That's what I really like." As he listened, the pastor thought, "Maybe he's right. Maybe we spend too much time on the music. I could give more attention to the preaching of the Word."

After the second man left, the pastor was confused. He had been confronted with two different opinions that both probably represented the feelings of others in the church. Wanting to adequately minister to everyone, he was torn. Then, suddenly, he felt he had the answer. Of course! God had sent *both* of those men to him that morning so he would be sensitive to *everybody's* opinion!

As I listened to the pastor finish his story, he turned to the blackboard behind him and drew two long vertical lines — one on the far left, and one on the far right. He pointed out that the line on the left represented the ritualistic and solemn worship that takes place in many traditional, liturgical churches. He explained that he did not feel that was what God wanted in his church. He felt that a dryness prevailed in many of "these kinds" of churches, which stifled the joy and presence of God.

He then pointed to the line on the far right, calling it a representation of churches that endorse "overly exuberant" worship. Vague references were made to his personal opinions of certain "excesses." He voiced his disapproval and told us he felt that it was out of order in the church.

Then, with a broad smile of satisfaction, he drew a new line — right down the middle of the board. He announced that *this* was where the church needed to stay in her worship time with the Lord. Not too grim, not too wild — just somewhere in between. There had to be *balance*. In consideration for the personal tastes of all the members of the church, compromise was necessary to insure unity.

As he made his proclamation, I felt extremely saddened. I became immediately disturbed that this pastor apparently had not asked the Lord how *He* wanted to be worshiped. In addition, there seemed to be a complete lack of concern for wholeheartedness in worship and for the ongoing love relationship Jesus desired with each person in that church. I felt that what this pastor proposed was not balance; rather, it was an attempt to appease the Michals and bind the Davids in one fell swoop (see 2 Samuel 6:20-21).

Balance is a deceitful concept in the church. In our best efforts to do the "acceptable," we can draw the line on both extremes, only to plant ourselves squarely in a patch of mediocrity. Because society thrives on being fickle — and the culture of our churches is no exception — the definition of what balance entails is always based on the perspective and opinion of each individual. There is no real standard. Therefore, one who is still clinging to what was considered "balance" ten years ago is probably foolishly out of sync today.

Many claim to have balance in their ministries by declaring that they preach "right down the middle of the road." Some pastors are determined not to go too far to the right for fear of falling into the ditch. But if he goes too far to the left, the pastor could fall into the ditch on that side. Soon, he is so caught up in avoiding the ditches that he preaches half-baked half-truths. He is paralyzed from moving forward, and he becomes overly critical of others whom he considers to be "ditch ministers" — those who preach anything different from his own narrow conceptions.

We cannot dilute doctrinal absolutes, but what is most often fiercely defended is opinion and personal preference. Different approaches and callings should not automatically shove our brother into a ditch. When we begin drawing lines and setting boundaries for the Holy Spirit, we box Him in, and we lose the ability to fully surrender to Him. He is not allowed to tell us to say or do anything that might be out of that box.

The "doctrine of balance" is taught nowhere in Scripture. *Attaining balance is not the same thing as attaining the will of God. Balance* is nothing more than a parking lot, where we park perfectly between the lines and sit on our positions. *The will of God* is not a parking lot: it is a highway that is always stretching out further than our personal horizons. We cruise along, and when the Lord speaks, sometimes we've got to change lanes, slow down, speed up or take a curve. We stay in the parameters of His Word and listen to His voice, and we will continue to move forward in His will, as long as we stay in His "lane." The Lord is constant, but His will does not cause us to stagnate in a parking lot. He does not change, but He *does* move. If we want to be in His will, we've got to move with Him, not park on our own perceptions.

The Bible is full of saints who were persecuted for their boldness and unconventional ways. The Lord nearly always asked them to do things that seemed unreasonable and "out of balance" at the time. Virtually all the heroes of the faith had a hint of insanity in them, particularly if we weigh their words and actions against the standards of their day. In fact, Jesus was the worst offender of all. Neither have God's ways conformed to our present-day norms. He is still looking for those who will be radical for Him.

Our goal should not be a balance birthed out of our own perceptions, but our highest obedience to God and an absolute submission of our wills to His. Self-defined balance will only lead us to legislate the work of the Lord in our lives. He will be glorified through us only by our complete obedience to Him.

The balance that prevails in the lukewarm church is one that is forever juggling the opinions of the "religiously correct." Being successful means discovering a harbor that keeps us at port and in the "safe" realm. We are destined to stagnate there if we will not venture out into the vast sea God has for us. We cannot be caught in the balance when the Holy Spirit sovereignly begins to be poured out. We will likely fight to preserve the balance and ignorantly run from the rain.

Many of the cries for balance in recent years were born from insecurity that the church is just not ready

85

to handle the power of the Holy Spirit or properly discern when the enemy interjects distractions. The battle rages over whether to corral the sheep or let them run completely free. What is needed is not a mixture of both, but a strong breed of leadership who will provide order without control, and promote liberty without allowing abuse. Hebrews 5:14 says that by *"reason of use"* our *"senses"* are *"exercised to discern both good and evil."* Leaders who have led their ministries from a presumption of balance have numbed their own senses and will be in dire straits to hear the voice of the Lord should they suddenly be faced with an outpouring that doesn't fit their criteria.

God wants leaders who will be willingly and joyfully afflicted with "spiritual amnesia." That is, they will subject themselves to being purged of preconceptions the modern church has attributed to the Lord's ways. They will be hard-pressed to remember what ought to happen in "normal" church. They will be stripped of all former landmarks of balance and social acceptability. They will be freed from human constraints that would quench the Spirit, and they will help the crippled church jump the hurdles of preconceived notions.

God is seeking a people who, like the apostles in Acts, will face the unprecedented fiercely standing on the Word of God, yet they will know His voice implicitly. They will not become an unrighteous authority that imposes legalistic standards, but they will be a righteous authority that provides an atmosphere for perfect order. The Lord's own endorsement of their authority will come as the absolute weakness of their flesh is unveiled, revealing their absolute dependence on Him. They will be known as a people who can do nothing of themselves; therefore, the glory of God will be all the more magnificent seen through them.

CHAPTER 10

EMBRACING THE COMFORT AND FEAR OF GOD

*I*n order to fervently abide with Jesus, we must be able to discern between godly comfort and ungodly complacency. The voice of the *Comforter* and the voice of carnal *comfort* are not the same. The voice of comfort, which is complacency, is an influence that will weigh you down every time you attempt a high endeavor. As soon as you purpose to climb a mountain, the voice of carnal comfort will become a hundred-pound backpack that you must carry with you as you try to ascend. It will say, "Oh, look how much pain you're in. Just rest here a while. God loves you so much — He couldn't require any more than this. Look around — you're already so much higher up than everyone else."

The voice of the *Comforter* — the Holy Spirit, who fills us with the peace of God — will never talk you out of a higher call. The true Comforter can simultaneously lead you into the midst of a fire while being your strength to endure it. First Corinthians 14:3 speaks of three results of the word of the Lord — *edification*, *exhortation* and *comfort*. That's how the Holy Spirit speaks to us so that we might do the Father's will. These words imply a "building up," as in the building of a house — an encouraging, a beseeching, a sustaining. They suggest that the Holy Spirit is like a coach, applauding for us to keep going and not give up. He's the One who is in us to empower us to do things that we could not possibly do in our own strength. He is always helping us to press on. Yes, the Holy Spirit is gentle in His leadings, but He is very definite in His purpose. He will *never* tell you to sit in a lukewarm bath.

Carnal comfort is not just about feeling nice and cozy. It's also about getting our essential needs met, and part of that is necessary and practical. The danger comes when the enemy or our own flesh fights to convince us that other comforters can meet our needs better than God can. Anything that serves as a substitute for God's spiritual provision in our lives is a false comforter.

If the devil cannot make inroads in our lives with false comfort, he will try to lead us into false fear. We are caught in false fear when we fear circumstances or men rather than trust God. Proverbs 29:25 says, *"The fear of man brings a snare, but whoever trusts in the LORD shall be safe."* Once we begin to revere anyone above the Lord, we are no longer secure in Him. We make decisions based on what we think other people want, rather than on what God is saying. Essentially, those people become our Lord. We may not ask people for their opinions, and they may not even be trying to control us. But out of our need to be accepted and admired, we can perpetuate a "people-pleasing" campaign based on what we believe would make them happy. Jesus should be the sole recipient of our "pleasing." After all, the Scriptures do say, *"When a man's ways please the LORD, He makes even his enemies to be at peace with him"* (Proverbs 16:7).

As we fear what men think of us, we then set the courses of our lives to please them instead of God. Paul said, *"If I still pleased men, I would not be a bondservant of Christ"* (Galatians 1:10). Those who have found themselves caught in the middle, trying to serve both God and man, cannot be purely devoted to the Lord. It is with this lack of tenacity that the lukewarm spirit can easily operate.

Sometimes there is manipulation exerted by a minister that requires those under him to be so focused on his vision that people downplay their own relationships with the Lord in order to serve "the man of God." There are undoubtedly those who take advantage of people who have a true servant's heart and use them for their own gain. But there are also those who choose — out of their own free will — to place a minister so high on a pedestal that their personal passion for the Lord is all but extinguished. This is not always the minister's fault. Many gifted ministers are besieged by persons who become dependent on them to act as their "high priests" and hear from God for them. Some people are anxious to serve a man of position, and then they completely allow their spiritual temperature to rise or fall based on the personal favor they receive or on the success of that ministry.

Churches have their own form of idol worship. We have forgotten — or maybe we've never known — how to fear God alone. We cannot supplant *His* Kingship in favor of a temporal "king." Also, the Lord does not want us to fear Him through mere knowledge of His historic demonstrations of wrath and judgment. To know Him only in that way would make Him seem distant and unapproachable. God reveals Himself to us daily, even though it is not necessarily in the pomp and majesty of a visible throne. He wants us to know Him in the full range of His many attributes, from lovingkindness to righteous wrath. We cannot negate the fear of the Lord. If we don't know the full breadth of His character, we don't really know Him.

Proverbs 9:10 says, *"The fear of the LORD is the beginning of wisdom,"* and Proverbs 15:33 says, *"The fear of the LORD is the instruction of wisdom."* In other words, fear comes first, then wisdom. We cannot hope to use our own wisdom to figure out how to fear God. Godly fear is the foundation of our ability to understand all the ways of God. Without the fear of the Lord, we can have no wisdom.

The fear of God is an unpopular topic in the lukewarm church, as outright fear and reverence bares our souls and ultimately calls for a reaction of unrestrained worship. Those who encountered the Lord in the Scriptures were awestruck and prostrated themselves before Him. In Revelation 1:17, even the Apostle John, who knew the Lord intimately on earth, immediately fell to the ground when Jesus appeared to him.

In fact, John states, *"I fell at His feet as dead."* The Lord then had to reassure him to not be afraid. This was the same man who had been so close to Jesus that he had lovingly laid his head on His breast!

If we willingly open ourselves up to the fear of God, we are making ourselves available for humbling activities like bowing, crying and lying "as if dead" at His feet. Someday, the fear of God will invade every person's heart like that! But ironically, most of these outward responses of holy fear would be offensive to a large cross-section of the contemporary church, because they are either considered either improper or emotionally immature. We have developed our own "acceptable" protocol for expressing our reverence to God, whether it is in our lifestyle choices or times of heartfelt worship. He tells us in Psalm 25:14, *"The secret of the LORD is with those who fear Him, and He will show them His covenant."* We are missing significant revelations in our relationship with the Lord if we do not have an understanding of what it means to fear Him.

In Mark 4:35-41, the disciples had a dual encounter with both the comfort and the fear of God. Jesus lay asleep in the boat as a storm arose, and the disciples began to fear for their lives. That was human fear, not the fear of God. But they called out to Jesus, *"Teacher, do You not care that we are perishing?"* (Mark 4:38).

Did you notice what they called Him? Teacher. They

had already seen Him perform miracles, but Mark records that earlier that day Jesus had taught extensively. "Teacher" was an honorable title to give Him, but did they still not "get it"? In crying out for their lives, was their primary focus on Jesus as their *teacher*? Did they not know what precious cargo was asleep in their boat? If He was only a teacher, they certainly had every reason to fear death. However, if He was the Master of the waves, then they were perfectly safe.

Jesus spoke to the storm and said, *"Peace, be still!"* (Mark 4:39). And what was the reaction? Now the disciples who had just feared for their safety *"feared exceedingly"*! This time, it was the fear of God. Jesus brought His protective comfort into that boat and delivered them from their situation. Yet, at the same time, His power also brought godly fear and a new slice of revelation of Jesus' true identity, that He indeed was God.

We can't go on calling Jesus just a good teacher or keep Him as a baby on a Christmas card. Neither is He a holy paramedic for us to call on in emergencies. We cannot embrace what we like about His comfort without seeing Him for the awesome King of Kings that He is. At the same time, the healthy kind of fear and reverence we carry for Him should remind us that He loves us implicitly and is willing to demonstrate His power on our behalf.

As we grow in true comfort and fear of God, the hand of the Lord fits the two perfectly together in our lives. If we are lacking in submission to the fear of God and cannot discern the voice of the real Comforter, we will have no ability to live holy lives. If we allow Him to sensitize our spiritual senses, they will be sharpened to respond to Him. It is the only way that we can really know Him.

CHAPTER 11

UNHOLY TOLERANCE

*I*n our quest for the true passion of God, we need to realize that our passion for Him is based on more than the strength of our holy pursuit. Being lukewarm is more than a lack of total abandonment to God. *A lukewarm heart is not only determined by indifference to the Lord, but also by tolerance of evil.* Indifference will, obviously, kill our ardent pursuit of God, but unholy tolerance causes us to shun His highest purposes for the Church.

If we develop even a base tolerance of evil, we then become excusing and hardened to sin — even our own. As a result, the joints in the Body of Christ become loosened because we will inevitably become equally unconcerned about the spiritual state of our brothers and sisters in Christ. We will no longer bear their burdens or care enough to correct them in love where there is a need. The God-ordained covenant we are called to keep with one another is exchanged for the humanistic philosophies of "live and let live" and "every man for himself."

If we continue living outside of personal account- ability and responsibility in relationships, we will fall captive to the prevailing principalities and powers sent upon entire churches and cities. The enemy often ac- complishes this without the church ever recognizing her own guilt. If we choose to do nothing, then we have, in fact, made a perilous and sinful choice. The lukewarm spirit deceptively presents indifference and tolerance as passive and even "humanitarian" choices, all the while veiling the dangerous repercussions of those choices. Psalm 36:4 makes this statement about the wicked: *"He does not abhor evil."* If that is a charge of sin against the ungodly, then what does God say about His own children who will not abhor — reject or loathe — evil?

The destructive success of the enemy hinges on his ability to convince us to continue in our tolerance. When we do not draw battle lines, the territory is un- claimed, and evil is waiting in the wings, ready to take over. When we find unholy tolerance in a Christian, his life will always reflect a resistance to the annihila- tion of evil. That may sound harsh, but if we refuse to acknowledge the opposition, are we not also allowing him to come and reign among us?

Tolerance for Satan's kingdom births a hesitancy to be committed to building God's Kingdom. The true work of the Lord never stands opposed. If we are not willing to take a stand, then even our highest intentions to build will soon give way to defeat. In Luke 16:16, Jesus says that as the Kingdom of God is preached, "everyone is pressing into it" by way of an offensive move. This pressing in calls for decisive movement. The Lord also says that *"The violent take it by force"* (Matthew 11:12). We take an aggressive position against the powers of the enemy whenever we purpose to despise anything that opposes the finished work of the cross.

When believers forsake their entitled authority and allow someone else to assume that position, they become vulnerable to unrighteous control. We are not to give others permission to dictate our lives, nor are we to come under bondage any person. Yet such a situation can occur when we simply avoid conflict and fail to take a stand.

First Kings talks about an evil queen named Jezebel. Even though her husband, King Ahab, was the sovereign leader, she began to impose her evil desires on the kingdom and override his authority. When a certain man, Naboth, refused to sell his vineyard to Ahab, Jezebel appealed to her husband by saying, *"You now exercise authority over Israel! Arise, eat food, and let your heart be cheerful; I will give you the vineyard of Naboth the Jezreelite"* (1 Kings 21:7). She proceeded to use the king's name and seal on letters to the elders of the city and orchestrated a plot to bring false accusations against Naboth. These brought a charge of blasphemy, which called for his death by stoning, and the subsequent release of the property Ahab desired.

The Hebrew meaning of *Naboth* is "fruits." When we, like Ahab, seek to expand our borders by trying to acquire fruits that are not legally ours, or things God has not told us we can have, we will be met with a denial of those things. If we are not careful, "Jezebel" will rise up in our lives to unrighteously grant us our desires. When Naboth was dead, Jezebel encouraged Ahab to go and take possession of his vineyard. Then Elijah the prophet declared that Ahab had sold himself *"to do evil in the sight of the LORD"* and prophesied calamity on his whole house (see 1 Kings 21:21-22).

Jezebel already had a reputation, as she had massacred God's prophets and promoted the worship of Baal. Not only was Ahab willing and tolerant for her to continue her evil, but the people of his kingdom had become so tolerant of Jezebel that when it came down to a showdown between the God of Elijah and Baal, they were unable to voice loyalty to either. First Kings 18:21 states:

> *Elijah came to all the people, and said, "How long will you falter between two opinions? If the LORD is God, follow Him; but if Baal, follow him."* **But the people answered him not a word.**

The people were so paralyzed by her control that they were no longer capable of making up their own minds or discerning the one true God for themselves.

Anyone who uses manipulation in order to gain unlawful authority in another person's life is taking on the attributes of Jezebel. Such a person is dictating his or her own desire into a situation and circumventing the wisdom of the Lord. This kind of control can send an entire ministry off course, just as Jezebel's control did to Ahab's kingdom.

Jezebel was definitely not a Proverbs 31 woman, but the permission she had to operate came from the king himself! He was the absolute ruler; therefore, he too was ultimately to blame for her evil actions. Not only was Ahab the king, but he was also her husband, which gave him personal rulership over her from that perspective as well. However, he failed to exercise that authority under either role. Ahab was tolerant and allowed evil to continue unchallenged. As a result, Elijah pronounced God's judgment upon him.

As children of the most high God, we walk in the authority He has given us as believers. Every one of us has a kingdom to maintain, whether it is a household, a job situation or a ministry. We, too, are faced with Jezebels who will entice us to sit back, compromise and let someone else do the driving or let sin continue around us. For all Jezebel's notorious evil, the only power she ever truly had is what Ahab allowed her to have. She was little more than a wicked, hungry scavenger who only picked up the authority that had been dropped. Ahab was not forced, but coerced, into cooperation with her. He was seduced into being tolerant of evil. Jezebel could not have operated without Ahab. If the legitimate authority refuses to be controlled or become complacent, then unrighteous authority cannot gain a foothold.

Those who are lukewarm and tolerant may welcome strong advice and sharp "spiritual" input, because it takes the pressure off one who is indecisive and noncommittal. Such flattering help is attractive, and God is often credited with bringing these highly devoted people into one's life. If we walk in that lukewarm tolerance, it is almost guaranteed that someone stronger in their convictions will eventually control us, because we need strong convictions to make decisions. If we don't have them, we let someone else do it for us. The "victim" easily lays down his weak spiritual state and bows to what looks godly — but isn't — simply because he is too indifferent to make choices. We will either listen to the Lord's voice, see our error and repent, or we will be manipulated into allowing a false strength to embrace us. That kind of "strength" promises comfort but brings a binding weakness.

The possibility exists for each of us to be cast in the role of a Jezebel or an Ahab, if Satan is directing a scenario in which one of us seems right for the part. Many who walk in what they believe to be true meekness and humility believe that they could never become a Jezebel. Yet, as Ahab, they can play the most important part in toppling true authority in the church. Where control, manipulation, power plays and unrighteous leadership run rampant, Ahab has surely laid a strong foundation for their existence. He must be dethroned. We must resist those tolerant, lukewarm inclinations to allow sin in the camp. We cannot let Jezebel build her own kingdom over us.

One way the church falls into this trap is by refusing to enforce New Testament discipline. Many people tend to embrace the platitude "We just need to love everybody." Novices and believers of questionable character are often allowed to take leadership positions because discrimination seems inconsistent with the Christian acceptance we promote. The church turns its head the other way when there is a problem, because we want to be tolerant and give everyone the benefit of the doubt — after all, who's perfect anyway? We fear that we will be looked down on as judgmental if we enforce godly principles. If someone in the church is hurt by the actions of another, the church doesn't want to get involved. In fact, the injured party is often condemned for his lack of forgiveness. Any person who wants to gain scriptural resolution of an issue is considered to be "stirring up strife" and is made to feel unwelcome. There is an unwillingness to allow confrontation; instead, our churches propagate a false "unity" through silence.

Matthew 18 gives detailed instructions on how to deal with someone who has committed an offense, but that scriptural pattern for discipline is often discarded as harsh, even though it is the Word of God. Modern Laodiceans do not want anyone around with the audacity to challenge the status quo. These attitudes are seeds that can lead to spiritual abuse and wrong types of control. The devil will continue to steal ground and build his strongholds. Pretty soon, others will start "coming out of the woodwork" when it becomes obvious that the church has no standards to uphold and the Scriptures are not honored.

When we walk in genuine love for our brothers and sisters, we will not maintain an attitude of toleration toward their sin. We are called to be instruments who edify and encourage each other, and if a brother or sister's spiritual health is a true concern, we will not stand by while he or she commits spiritual suicide. If someone were holding a gun to his head, would you say, "Well, if that's what you want, go ahead and shoot"? But we see the same thing happening spiritually in the church on a regular basis. As the Lord wholeheartedly endorses the *restoration* of those who have fallen into sin, He just as adamantly opposes the continuing *toleration* of sinful conduct:

> *But we command you, brethren, in the name of our Lord Jesus Christ, that you withdraw from every brother who walks disorderly and not according to the tradition which he received from us.*
>
> 2 Thessalonians 3:6

> *Reject a divisive man after the first and second admonition, knowing that such a person is warped and sinning, being self-condemned.*   Titus 3:10-11

> *It is actually reported that there is sexual immorality among you …. And you are puffed up, and have not rather mourned, that he who has done this deed might be taken away from you. … When you are gathered together, along with my spirit, with the power of our Lord Jesus Christ, deliver such a one to Satan for the destruction of the flesh,*

*that his spirit may be saved in the day of the Lord
Jesus.*   1 Corinthians 5:1-5

In our society, where we want to promote the idea that God loves the sinner even though He hates the sin, we have allowed tremendous compromise to enter the church. We have adopted the worldly notion that it is unfair to saddle a believer with the conviction of Scripture. But when we do not operate in the truth that sets men free, we are not operating in the mercy of God. We are leading some on the primrose path to hell, while upholding their sin as a personal right.

The reason Paul dealt with sin so strongly is that he knew the end result of letting it go on. There was an admonition to "cut off" the unrepentant sinner, not as an end in itself, but in the hope that he would be grieved by the separation and come to grips with his sin. If someone has become calloused to the Lord, then a severe humbling is sometimes the only way to bring him back. Condoning his sin and allowing him to remain part of the church only gives him the liberty to stay in deception and become more insensitive. He then becomes like a spoiled child who makes his own rules, and the Word of God becomes void in his life.

The harshness of the Lord's dealing is not only required for the sinner, but it protects others in the church. If impressionable young believers see others in willful, excused sin, they can become confused and even think that the Lord might condone such behavior. The removal of such culprits also prevents others in the Body of Christ from being victimized by additional offenses, and in extreme cases may even protect them from physical harm.

By far, the easiest sin for us to tolerate is our own. We are beyond deliverance if we will not confess our sin to the Lord, because we are often the only ones who know the filth that exists within us. Outward sins of rebellion and immorality should be renounced, of course, but often, others know about those sins, or natural circumstances will expose them and bring them to light. Our hidden, secret sins may be the most corrosive. These inward sins assault our spirits, yet if they continue unchecked, we will never be brought to our knees. Sins like "harmless" thoughts of deception, pride and compromise can drive giant wedges into our relationships with God without our even fully recognizing them.

Those who are not involved in "major" sins like drugs, pornography, adultery or gambling often live according to a standard of comparison, which they believe gives their spiritual walks a "clean bill of health." As 1 John 1:8 says, *If we say that we have no sin, we deceive ourselves, and the truth is not in us.* If we are really growing in our relationships with the Lord, our hatred for sin should also grow. As we mature in the revelation of the reality of abundant life, we should become more soberly aware of the death that we have escaped.

Tolerance of sin in others and in ourselves is an indication that we are willing to passively excuse what God has clearly condemned. Dwelling under the umbrella of the full counsel of the Lord and coming into agreement with His Word as absolute authority increases the level of conviction on our lives. As our sensitivity to that conviction increases, so do our opportunities to walk in pureness of heart. The Lord promises in Matthew 5:8 that *"the pure in heart ... shall see God."* We cannot expect to have purity without cleansing, and we cannot be cleansed without surrendering in repentance.

When we choose to tolerate evil, we are setting up roadblocks that detour us from our course to knowing the Lord more intimately. When we come into agreement with Him against His enemy, we will also share in His victory.

CHAPTER 12

WAGING WAR IN LAODICEA

*M*any believers have been lulled in a lukewarm attitude toward the evil that is out to destroy them. In 2 Corinthians 2:11, Paul speaks of not being ignorant of the devices of Satan. Often, we do not recognize our enemy. We never expect him to come in the ways he does, and he is very good at masking his blame behind human flesh. That is why the Scriptures remind us that *"we do not wrestle against flesh and blood"* (Ephesians 6:12); that is where we first try to fight our battles. We can never be victorious by simply fighting on that battleground. If Satan can keep us sidetracked enough to stay on fleshly turf, we will become weary and even more susceptible to his attack.

While involved in foreign wars, American soldiers learned to have a healthy distrust of children in battle zones. The enemy used them as clever decoys, tying explosives to them or training them in various warfare tactics. Children can infiltrate an armed defense in a way that an adult enemy soldier never could. How many times does the devil come to us as that little "child," hoping that we will not suspect that he is trying to gain entrance into our lives?

In order to subdue the enemy, we must first be subdued ourselves. We will only be able to walk in the Spirit when we stop lugging our flesh around, trying to wield it as though we could stave off the enemy. Any contribution we make in the flesh, trying to "help" God, only dilutes His power moving through us. We walk in the authority of our callings, but our dependence still must remain in Him. We do not need to run *from* the enemy, but we still must remember to run *to* God: *"The name of the LORD is a strong tower; the righteous run to it and are safe"* (Proverbs 18:10).

Any area in the life of a church that is dampened by a lukewarm spirit is crippled in its effectiveness, but a church that clearly refuses to wage war against the enemy of the cross sentences itself to a hard time in the penitentiary of oppression. Executing the Lord's judgments on the enemy is an honor granted to His saints (see Psalm 149:9). We should not shrink back in any way from enforcing the justice that God has entrusted to us.

Countries that are not at war still maintain military personnel, recruiting soldiers and training them for the possibility of deployment. Just the presence of a peacekeeping army protecting a nation's borders often insures that an enemy will not come and attack it.

Isn't it amazing that much of the church does not even adopt prevention as a viable necessity, even though the Body of Christ dwells alongside an enemy who is undeterred by the mere *threat* of our military strength? We have an enemy who never tires of trying to infiltrate our ranks and destroy the work of God. Sometimes his attack may come through an onslaught, but he is just as likely to work through inside espionage, slowly tearing apart the fabric of our church body.

The church that either ignores the enemy or believes it is immune just because its members have built something dedicated to God is wide open to attack. As much as possible, Satan prefers to work in ways that will do the most damage without revealing that he is the source of the problem. He desires to cause havoc without exposing the presence of his demonic influence. That way, the church becomes overly consumed with "people problems."

Every church has its own stance on spiritual warfare, but regardless of theological specifics, the lukewarm church will not forge ahead for the Kingdom of God because, at best, it only knows how to operate in a maintenance mode. The only spiritual warfare a lukewarm church knows how to wage is the desperate, defensive stance for survival after a major blow. Even then, removing the immediate threat is the one and only goal, not tracking down and rooting out the true source of the attack. Although there is room for plenty of diversity of personality and methods in an individual church, there is not room for serious delusion about the intent of our enemy. The devil is keenly aware that he has little time left to cause destruction. He is working furiously against a stopwatch while we sit back, thinking we have all the time in the world.

The most fundamental element we need to grasp is that we have no choice about whether or not we are in a battle. When we make the decision to follow the Lord, we are also drafted for a lifelong tour of duty in His army. We must know *what* we are fighting for and passionately love *whom* we are fighting for.

We each have a land of possession that contains the promises of God for our victory in this life. The Lord could just hand it over to us, but as with the Israelites, He uses the opposition we face to sharpen and to train us for our eternal service in His Kingdom. The Lord will deliver our enemy into our hands, but it is up to us whether he will stay or go.

The Lord is adamant about the total destruction of our enemy; our opponent is a ruthless killer. If we don't destroy the enemy, he will destroy us. David said, *"I have pursued my enemies and overtaken them; neither did I turn back again till they were destroyed"* (Psalm 18:37). Because Saul, who had sought to kill him, had chased David, he knew that there was a decided advantage to being the pursuer over having an enemy nipping at his heels.

Psalm 18 goes on to say, in verse 42, *"I beat them as fine as the dust before the wind; I cast them out like dirt in the streets."* We are to stomp on any remnant of the enemy's work in our lives so that he cannot regroup and come after us with it again. Any seeds of unresolved conflict with others — fear, rejection or bitterness — are all smelling salts that can revive the enemy's attack with a vengeance. We need to purge the enemy completely so that he will stay defeated.

Doubt is one major force that can keep us from ever seeing a battle through to completion. First Corinthians 9:26 says that we should not run with uncertainty, but we should run in such a way that we will win the prize. If we cannot pursue our enemy with the faith that he will meet his demise, then we would be better off not engaging him. We must have confidence that our God is not only powerful, but that His will has already been settled concerning our victory.

Remember, the enemy does not flee in response to our emotional zeal or anger. A fiery personality does not scare him, nor must he legally submit to yelling and empty accusation. People in some circles have a mistaken impression that the devil won't leave unless we come across like "tough guys" and show him who's boss. Ironically, sometimes that kind of personality can be found in one who is full of arrogance, full of pride and insensitivity, all of which are major hindrances in dealing with the demonic. Those characteristics are descriptive of our enemy, not of God! Neither should they be traits of God's servants, who are attempting to work on His behalf. We must separate the characteristics of a stereotypical "General Patton" from a real soldier of the Lord.

If we flaunt our "rank" in front of our enemy without a pure heart, it is like trying to lift weights without muscles. We have no true strength outside of our Christ-centered authority. The same David who killed

Goliath also told the Lord, *"Your gentleness has made me great"* (Psalm 18:35). Nothing in our personalities qualifies us for His authority. Isaiah 30:15 says that *"in quietness and confidence shall be your strength."* A lack of agitation or anxiety may actually indicate the presence of peace in a person and an assurance of faith. It should not automatically be mistaken for being lax or luke-warm about the works of the enemy. Some of the most "successful" times of personal deliverance I have observed gave very little time and attention to the devil. Loudly proclaiming our victory over someone who needs ministry does not necessarily result in deliverance or spiritual encouragement. Rather, it is the compassion of Jesus and knowing who we are in Him that will truly minister to a person's need. If our focus would be more on the restoration of that person's soul than on getting another "notch" in our belt, we would see the spotlight shine more on the Lord than on the ridiculous antics of the adversary. The extent to which we perform for the devil is not a gauge of our authority. The true test is whether we are bringing glory to God when we take up His authority. If not, it is not true ministry.

On the other hand, we need to remember that the havoc our enemy creates should rouse us to a *holy* anger. David says in Psalm 139:21-22, *"Do I not hate them, O LORD, who hate You? And do I not loathe those who rise up against You? I hate them with perfect hatred; I count them my enemies."* The Scriptures say that *"God is angry with the wicked every day"* (Psalm 7:11), and if we are in tune with His heart, then we will view His enemy the same way. Seeing someone's life wrecked by the enemy should make us angry, but our main focus should still be on the restoration of the wounded person.

In Nahum 3, the Lord rebukes the men of Nineveh for allowing the city to be "laid waste." In verse 13, He says, *"Surely, your people in your midst are women! The gates of your land are wide open for your enemies; fire shall devour the bars of your gates."* By calling them "women," the Lord was saying that they were unskilled, weak, timid, unable and unwilling to fight. (Consider the culture of the day and the fact that women were not trained to be warriors.) God is looking for His Church to rise up and take her place. Willful continuance in sin and lethargy can render us ineffective against the enemy. Other than that, only our own unwillingness to follow God's directions can deter us. Gender is no excuse — the Lord does not want *women* to be "women" either.

The Lord does not want us to hesitate to achieve decisive victory. How could He ever be glorified in hesitation? Sporadic warfare only invites the enemy to a cooperative exchange of power. In essence, it does little more than incite the enemy to manifest himself further, knowing that he won't be pursued to a full defeat. He can, therefore, use the little he has to keep fear and helplessness at our doors.

The Lord desires our warfare to be just as wholehearted as our worship. David was adept at both, and he is known for his profound passion in both realms. Psalm 144 illustrates this beautifully. In verse 1, David

115

praises the Lord who *"trains my hands for war, and my fingers for battle."* Then, in verse 9, he declares, *"I will sing a new song to You, O God; on a harp of ten strings I will sing praises to You."* The fingers that the Lord fine-tuned for battle were also the ones He anointed with skill to praise Him on the harp. David had the distinction of being a man after God's own heart. If we want to be the same, then we can expect God to draw us likewise into everything that concerns Him.

CHAPTER 13

BLESSINGS TO THE OVERCOMER

eing an overcomer is not just about that moment in your future when Jesus will say to you, "Well done! You overcame!" It is just as much about who you are right now, while you are in the process of living out your faith. *An overcomer is one who is already walking in the victory he has not yet attained.*

To those in Laodicea who would forsake their lukewarm state, the Lord promised, "*To him who overcomes I will grant to sit with Me on My throne, as I also overcame and sat down with My Father on His throne*" (Revelation 3:21). Because they had been so deeply blinded by their sin of compromise, it is possible that even after hearing the message directed to them, the Laodiceans still were unable to perceive the extent of their grave condition. It is likely that the journey out of their lukewarmness had to begin with a response to the convicting word of God alone, without their feeling an emotional agreement with the charges.

As opposed to the predictable, comfortable future they had planned, turning and repenting may have looked risky and downright scary. The required repentance would include a stage of refining and putting on a new righteousness that may have seemed attractive because it was the right thing to do, but it must have filled them with apprehension. Inevitably, they would have to look in God's mirror and face the reality of their wretchedness.

To overcome meant more than conquering their fears and compromise. It also meant facing the turmoil and persecution that would inevitably be stirred up by the enemy as they made the decision to dismantle the stronghold that they had helped him build. As Paul said, *"Yes, and all who desire to live godly in Christ Jesus will suffer persecution"* (2 Timothy 3:12). Newfound desire to follow the Lord completely would invite evil repercussions.

As Jesus granted the privilege of sitting on His throne to the overcomers in Laodicea, He added, *"as I also overcame and sat down with My Father on His throne"* (Revelation 3:21). For some reason, He identified Himself as having overcome in the *same way* that they would have to! Hebrews 4:15 says, *"For we do not have a High Priest who cannot sympathize with our weaknesses, but was in all points tempted as we are, yet without sin."* Jesus can certainly have compassion for every believer over the temptations that each may face, but how could He relate to what was prevalent in the church of Laodicea?

After Jesus was baptized by John the Baptist, He was led into the wilderness to be tested (see Matthew 4). After Jesus endured forty days of fasting, the devil came to tempt Him. It was a battle in which His true allegiances would be decided. Did He want bread or the Word of God? Did He want to test God in His power or stand in the assurance that He already possessed? Did He want all the kingdoms of the world or a Kingdom not of this world, which would only come through a cross?

First John 2:16 says: *"For all that is in the world — the lust of the flesh, the lust of the eyes, and the pride of life — is not of the Father but is of the world."* These were the things Jesus was tempted with, and the Laodicean church flirted with these very same temptations! After craving the taste of the world's comforts, they would have to go out to that wilderness and tell the devil "no" on all counts. The temptation would be even harder to overcome as the enemy had the perfect ammunition — their own fresh memories of a lukewarm religion they had been quite comfortable and satisfied in.

Another battle Jesus faced was in the Garden of Gethsemane, where He made the final decision to go to His death. This is where He embraced the Father's will at His own expense. Of course, He had to walk out the death march, but His will was already resolute and broken. Whoever is deemed worthy to sit

119

beside Jesus in Heaven will be broken on earth as He was. Jesus willingly left glory to lay down His life for us. Overcomers will put aside whatever glory they could attain in this world and willingly lay down their lives for Him.

One who has no physical comforts in this life and has little to look forward to other than an eternal home may see Jesus as their only hope and so be heavenly minded. The vision of Heaven may give them strength to make spiritual investments since they have no earthly wealth. The little they have in this world pales in the shadow of the riches of Heaven. It seems that it would be relatively easy to lay down a life that is poor and insignificant to gain an eternity beyond one's wildest imagination.

But like Jesus, the church of Laodicea had her own brand of glory to lay aside. She had wealth, goods and a comfortable lifestyle, not to mention a load of spiritual self-congratulations. We know all this was a tarnished glory — a poor substitute for the blessings of fullness in Christ. The glory of the spirit of comfort that the Laodiceans enjoyed made them "millionaires of the flesh." To not walk in that again would be like a rich man going to live on the street and never touching his bank account. The lukewarm spirit promised the luxury of spiritual ease and an esteem that their material prosperity continually affirmed.

God is not necessarily telling us to throw away everything we own and become paupers, living a life void of material blessings and basic provision. Nor is He telling us to deny ourselves spiritually from the abundance of teaching and opportunities in the church so that we won't take anything for granted. He is asking for something much more difficult. He is asking for people who are full from eating a huge feast of worldly blessing to sit down at the Lord's banquet table and eat of Him with ravenous hunger. We fill ourselves with what the world offers, then we somehow find room for the "better" things the church agenda has to offer, but by then we are so satisfied that we find we don't have room for the best things of God Himself. We are not hungry for Him anymore. We are complacent and lukewarm.

As we open ourselves to be surrendered to His presence, we are stirred with a yearning to be with Him on His throne. To be overcomers, we must follow this desire for Him wherever it takes us. We must commit to a kind of passion that will carry a cross. We must submit to the One we have not seen, but love. We must worship Him in all awareness of His holiness and worth. We must seek Him totally, knowing that we cannot yet behold the beauty of the face we long to see. As we joyfully give all He asks, we will humbly receive all He gives. We will be on fire and never be quenched, and *we will overcome.*

CHAPTER 14

THE FOUNDERING FLOCK

*I*t stands to reason that lukewarm sheep will flock together; they make each other comfortable. Those who would justify that spiritual condition will seek out an unchallenging atmosphere where they will be undisturbed. Likewise, pastors and leaders who have a Laodicean mentality will attract those who feel they are "safe" under such passive leadership.

The choices people make while sitting on a church pew have the capacity to change their lifestyles, as well as their eternal destinies. A minister should take that burden with him every time he accepts the pulpit. People will not receive from someone they don't trust, so if he has gained their confidence, then his words can have a substantial impact.

As long as leadership will identify with or tolerate lukewarm Christianity, this condition will never be fully addressed in the church. Because of the position of trust the sheep award to most pastors, many will not even attempt to discern a negative state in themselves. They expect their pastor to warn and protect them from any encroaching blind spots. However, the pastor cannot do that if he is caught in the same lukewarm snare. Besides, the pressure of increasing "numbers" and pleasing others may mold a pastor into a hireling who cares more about keeping his job than he does about laying down his life for the sheep.

God rebuked the inept leaders of Israel thus: *"They all look to their own way, every one for his own gain, from his own territory"* (Isaiah 56:11).

A leader's mere slant of words can drive lukewarmness deeper into the life of a church. First, watering down truth to cool possible offenses can defuse the original conviction and revelation that God wants to bring. Second, hype and repeated exaggeration can quench the expectancy and faith of a congregation. When people always hear, "This sermon is going to change your life forever," disappointment follows if things do not materialize as expected. Understandably, people lose their expectancy, and complacency sets in. Third, making flowery, presumptuous promises concerning the impact of future programs or church growth can kill the unity a church must have in order to implement new vision.

If a shepherd is lukewarm, the truly hungry sheep will begin to starve. They will eventually leave and seek another pasture or become disillusioned with the church and be lost. The lukewarm sheep will stay and continue to be blindly comfortable.

There is a silent agreement between the lukewarm shepherd and his sheep that they will go no further with God than the corral they have erected. They operate under the false caution that they could get "too far out" in spiritual things and not be able to get back. This spiritual fallacy has the same effect as the ancient fear that the earth was flat. Myths were circulated that if someone followed the horizon far enough, he would fall off the end of the world. Artists depicted dragons, fire and other such dangers to be awaiting the brash sailor who would dare defy the confines of the earth.

Have you ever thought about the fact that Satan not only brought unfounded fear to people, but that he also hindered them from enjoying the natural resources God had provided for the whole earth? Taking this thought a step further, surely this deception delayed worldwide evangelism by many years.

The lukewarm church is afraid to move at all because she does not know how far she can walk toward that unfamiliar horizon before finding herself caught in the "Twilight Zone." If we are truly following the Lord, however, we will not stray away and fall off some obscure deep end. We can only do that by bowing to the enemy or to our own flesh, and that is what the lukewarm church is doing anyway! If our spiritual journey is grounded in the Lord, we can depend on the faithfulness of the Holy Spirit — that His "gravity" will keep our feet firmly on the ground wherever we walk. As we go "full circle" (just like our globe), we discover that the final destination of every trek of true revelation begins and ends at the same place — at the foot of the cross and in the person of Jesus.

Any spiritual influence works through the personalities of those who are affected by it, and the lukewarm spirit is no exception. But, by and large, resistance to the Holy Spirit is universally very prevalent among the lukewarm. Only the Lord really knows who is resisting Him. But those who verbalize their pride, who consider themselves independent of the need for the Lord and who consider themselves "rich" are printing their own labels.

If, like the Laodiceans, we become the "king of the hill" in our own little world, the perception we have of our kingdom will always be bigger than it is in reality. If hundreds admire us, we assume thousands know about us and are praising the anointing on our lives. If God has sent us to a couple of foreign countries, we now can claim to have an international, worldwide ministry. We assume that exposure equals endorsement, and we forget that our Savior was born in a stable without any media.

Spiritual "fatherhood" medals or "credit" for certain streams or movements are often bestowed on individuals in the Body of Christ, and we have Christian "experts" on every subject. Giving honor where honor is due is good and right, but reputations are often puffed up in order to sell books or fill conferences, and many truly anointed men and women of God have become obscured within the huge army of those who trumpet their claims to be anointed. I wonder how many would want to be counted among the anointed if there was a national law that all "anointed" ministers would be put to death.

The worst liability of a high reputation is that if we believe our own press, we will lose the persistence to run our race to a victorious completion, and never do the mightier things God has called us to do. If we think we have already reached the top of the mountain, we will spend precious time standing in awe of our own accomplishments.

Isolation can feed our pride, giving us an elitist attitude that will keep us out of circulation with those who would point out our weaknesses. Proverbs 27:17 says, *"As iron sharpens iron, so a man sharpens the countenance of his friend."* When you sharpen something, you grate against it with a friction that takes the dull edge off of it. A real friend is one who will say the hard things that make for a keen spirit. If we isolate ourselves, even within a small circle of friends, we may still suffer due to the narrow thinking of the group, and we will become no sharper for it.

Lukewarm churches often emphasize a "fruits over gifts" mentality, yet excel at neither. Fruits can be easily imitated by our own efforts, so lukewarm people are comfortable with fruits. The presence and power of God is often shelved with the justification that belief has reached a more elite realm if the Lord is not "having to" manifest Himself. The words of Jesus to Thomas that a blessing awaits those who "have not seen, yet believe" — can become an implied motto. It gives the masked impression of living in a higher level of faith.

As this consensus is adopted, sometimes the Holy Spirit is seen as two separate entities — the mature, angelic spirit who brings sweet fruits of charity and temperance, and His selfish, immature, evil twin, the frivolous, sloppy gift-giver. The "wise and intelligent, levelheaded Christians" dedicated to virtue and integrity choose the higher purpose — the fruits, while the "emotional, empty-headed droolers" selfishly go for the grab bag — the gifts.

However, the gap can be closed on our stereotypes if we will remember that everything the Holy Spirit gives IS a gift. Fruits are not honorable and gifts shameful. Fruits are not for the strong and gifts for the weak. Fruits are not achievement badges of our own virtue; they are supernatural attributes of God, which are mercifully manifested through human flesh. If you meet a patient Buddhist, do you recognize that patience as a fruit of the Spirit? If you know a Hindu who diligently prays and never forsakes his faith, do you attribute that to the Holy Spirit fruit of faithfulness? No.

It has often been said, "Gifts are *given*, and fruit is *grown*." I can't find that in Scripture. They are both *given*, and, likewise, we *grow* in both of them. Our gifts mature, and our fruit matures. As we receive everything the Holy Spirit desires to do in and through us, we will walk in the harmony of both fruits and manifestations of power. Jesus did, and His disciples followed

His example. The compassion they had for people enabled them to effectively minister healing, deliverance, salvation and prophetic wisdom into lives, who not only received miracles but also were touched by the highest fruit of the love of God.

Some churches that are willing to embrace the gifts of the Spirit also have limitations and preferences. When I was first introduced to the power of God and became aware that the gifts were real and for today, I had the assumption that it was a package deal. If you believed in tongues, then healing, prophecy and the rest came along automatically. In my awkward innocence, I was initially shocked when I began to observe Charismatic believers attempting to dismantle the gifts, picking their favorites and discarding those that they did not understand or found offensive.

Although some stifle the works of the Spirit in selective ways, even more are completely closed to His power or to a relationship with Him in the first place. Once, as I was discussing the Holy Spirit with someone and sharing with her how He had made a profound difference in my prayer life and my ability to effectively minister to others, she informed me that she didn't need a deeper experience with Him. She felt that she was already a very strong Christian and that everything was fine the way it was. I wanted to ask her how we could possibly claim to be so much stronger than the apostles, everyone in the Upper Room, and all the churches in the New Testament. How is it that those who had the privilege of eye-witnessing Jesus in the flesh and the evidence of His resurrection were so "weak" that they needed a special outpour-ing of the Holy Spirit to get them going, and yet our faith today is considered leagues beyond that? Do we think we are already so full of God that we have the maturity to skip the enduing with power that was sought after and waited for by the early Church?

Our resistance to God is telling Him, "No thanks, I've got enough of You. I don't need to overdo it." The one who believes that asking to receive more of any-thing from the Lord is an admission of weakness is absolutely right. That's what He wants! But 2 Corin-thians 12:9 says that *"[His] strength is made perfect in weakness."* The Lord is saying that He will take the cup containing our weakness and fill it with His strength — then we will have His fullness. If the only time we acknowledge our weakness is when we have a crisis, then when that crisis is resolved, we will turn back to our resistance. We have only acknowledged that cir-cumstances can bring us to our knees; we have not acknowledged our inherent weakness.

The result of continued resistance is that we get used to a low level of relationship and power and begin to accept it as the norm. First John 2:27 says:

> *But the anointing which you have received from Him abides in you, and you **do not need that anyone teach you**; but as the same anointing teaches you concerning all things, and is true, and is not a lie, and just as it has taught you, you will abide in Him.*

If we are drawing on that anointing and pursuing

the Holy Spirit, He will guide us into truth and we will continue to grow and mature. However, if we are resisting His anointing, we will not learn from our true Teacher even if we are in church every time the doors are open. We instead are dull of hearing.

> *For though by this time you ought to be teachers,* **you need someone to teach you** *again the first principles of the oracles of God; and you have come to need milk and not solid food.* Hebrews 5:12

Wait! John said we don't need a teacher. However, the scripture from Hebrews implies not only the need for a teacher, but for a nursery school teacher! Apparently these believers had not drawn on the anointing readily available to them and had resisted and regressed to the point that they did not know how to interact with the Holy Spirit on the most foundational level anymore. We cannot decide to follow the Lord in a token way and plateau in the valley. If we do not keep walking, we will atrophy and eventually forget how to walk.

Resistance can be masked in the church by substituting "righteous activity" for the person of the Holy Spirit. Overemphasis on other areas is promoted to "fill" the space the Lord should be occupying. For example, preaching is wonderful and needed, but it should not be ninety-nine percent of everything that goes on in a church. Programs and support-type groups should not be introduced without establishing a primary emphasis on real New Testament ministry, and we should not propose to offer pure liturgy as a substitute for personal passion and worship.

The Laodicean church lived in the deception that she had "become wealthy," that is, increased with goods. Churches today collect buildings, programs, and tithing members. No matter how much we think we have done for God, we should be sobered by the words of Matthew 7:22-23:

> *Many will say to Me in that day, "Lord, Lord, have we not prophesied in Your name, cast out demons in Your name, and done many wonders in Your name?" And then I will declare to them, 'I never knew you; depart from Me, you who practice lawlessness!"*

I once heard someone say that we had better be careful not to presume that we will hear, "Well done, good and faithful servant," just because we have done the supernatural works of God on the earth. The people the Lord was talking to in this passage were not from "dead" churches without power; they were ones who practiced prophecy, deliverance and miracles. We can never align ourselves with the belief that we are doing God a favor and that He is subservient to our willingness to "help" Him. If we are privileged to serve Him, we must remember His admonition, *"When you have done all those things which you are commanded, say, 'We are unprofitable servants. We have done what was our duty to do'"* (Luke 17:10). We will never reach the point where we can impress God by doing more than He has commanded or given us the grace to do.

A lukewarm church depends on the kinds of props that will prevent total collapse without causing the people to hunger for something more. The goal is to keep them satisfied in their current state. Even promoting legalism can harden into a protective shield against spiritual passion because it feeds the pride of those who adhere to it. Legalism gives the church an ongoing list of "good works" that they can misappropriate to their credit. It is the pillar of the religious spirit that makes people feel secure in their own righteousness. Pharisees offer a "helpful" crutch by promoting past glory as the only glory. If any pockets of hunger arise in the church, they are put down by assurances that God is pleased to have a people who will believe without seeing and that they have already arrived on that higher plane of faith.

In his book, *Roadkill Seminary,* my friend Pastor Jeff Krall lists three characteristics of a ministry that has abandoned self-sufficiency and is aiming for the highest purposes of God. If a church is led by a minister who has a burning hunger to see God's people walk in close relationship with God, the Laodicean spirit will run out of room to operate.

First, if we want to be a church that is a fire pan for God, *"We cannot lead by consensus, but only by conviction."* We must be moved by the impression of the Holy Spirit and not by popularity vote. It is true that there is wisdom in a multitude of counselors, but there is no wisdom in an angry mob or an opinion poll. That is nothing more than "pooled ignorance." We need to know that the word of God dwells in those we prayerfully choose to advise us, and we need the assurance that their motives are pure.

Second, *"We cannot lead by persuasion, but only by authority."* We must abandon our need to have our own way even with the people who respect us and especially want to please us. "To persuade" is to talk someone into something that he or she did not originally want to do. Such a person is *seduced*, not brought into agreement. There needs to be agreement in the church that God's authority will be honored above all else when the leadership needs to bring forth what the Lord is commanding.

Third, *"we cannot lead by enthusiasm, but only by anointing."* Mere excitement does not sustain a church, and the more we depend on it and make it a habit, the less we will be willing to stand vulnerable before God's people before we will use it. If we are ministering and don't feel that we are anointed, we can be tempted to pour the "oil of hype" over ourselves to stir things up. At that point, however, we have lost the direction of the Lord, and He will withdraw His blessing from what we are doing.

Today's church leaders need a new brand of courage, one that will give them the strength to both resist the lure of the lukewarm spirit and lead their sheep to greener pastures. I believe there are many foundering, who would eagerly follow the example of a man of God who dares to light a fire in the Church.

CHAPTER 15

FANNING THE FLAMES

he last statement Jesus makes in His message to Laodicea is: *"He who has an ear, let him hear what the Spirit says to the churches."* We all have a responsibility to listen to the Lord and heed His voice. But some in the Body of Christ are called to stand and fan the flames over present-day Laodicea, calling the overcomers to come forth and helping them to hear His voice. To those, I believe the Lord would say, "He who has a *voice*, let him *say* what the Spirit says to the churches."

One significant hindrance to speaking the word of the Lord in Laodicea is that they are not asking for it. They will be the last to say, "Tell us what the Lord shows you." In Isaiah 30, God speaks of His *"rebellious people ... who say to the seers 'Do not see,' and to the prophets, 'Do not prophesy to us right things; speak to us smooth things, prophesy deceits.'"* The lukewarm also want to hear "smooth things," and they want their present state left unchallenged. But we must not shrink back from the undiluted word of the Lord. If it is received, the speaking of truth opens a door for repentance and restoration. When Jesus spoke truth to the woman at the well, He did not bring up her wonderful qualities; He exposed her sin. But she was ministered to and edified as she realized that the Lord was interested enough in her to know and to care about the personal details of her life.

The fresher the word, the more likely it is that it will be rejected in Laodicea. Some who claim to know where the "cloud" is moving have not necessarily heard from God for themselves; rather, they are only repeating what they have read or heard from others. If you are one step behind the cloud, you are not under the cloud. Just because our tradition has "caught up" with what God was doing five years ago doesn't mean we are moving with the cloud now. We are still outside the camp. The lukewarm church needs to have a "now" word from God to accurately see where she stands.

In Romans 11:14, Paul expressed his desire to provoke the Jews to jealousy over salvation being brought to the Gentiles. He did not want to feed them knowledge, of which he had an abundance, but rather to ignite a hunger in them that would compel them to seek Christ. The goal, then, for any saint who wants to foster an abhorrence for Laodicea should be to provoke a jealousy in others that will cause them to yearn for more of the Lord. Ministers, especially, should seek to provoke hunger in people even more than to feed and satisfy them.

Those who speak over Laodicea should also be diligent. If we are *complacent* about praying against *complacency*, then, by our actions, we are just coming into agreement with what we are praying against! When Israel fought the second battle with Ai, the Lord promised Joshua a victory. But He had a condition — *"Stretch out the spear that is in your hand toward Ai, for I will give it into your hand"* (Joshua 8:18). Because Joshua was obedient, Ai was defeated. The reason, however, was that *"Joshua did not draw back his hand, with which he stretched out the spear, until he had utterly destroyed all the inhabitants of Ai"* (Joshua 8:26).

There is a similar incident in 2 Kings 13. King Joash came to the prophet Elisha's deathbed to inquire about his enemy, Syria. Elisha told him to take a bow and arrows and shoot out the window as a prophetic sign of Syria's demise. Then he told Joash to take the arrows and strike the ground with them. Joash chose to stop after only three strikes. Elisha was angry because Joash had not continued as he should have. As a result of this failure to follow through in this prophetic action, God only granted him three successful strikes on Syria, which would not be sufficient to destroy it completely.

As we make prophetic proclamation over what is lukewarm in the church — and in ourselves — our fiercest enemy is that Laodicean voice that would cause us to stop before we have overcome. Like Joash, we could do damage, but our enemy will still be lurking around. Like Joshua, we must not let our arms grow weary. First Timothy 1:18 says that we should *"wage the good warfare"* according to the prophecies spoken over us. The Lord has promised us victory if we move confidently toward the battle and do not retreat from it. We must continue to say what God is saying.

Revelation 19:10 says that *"the testimony of Jesus is the spirit of prophecy."* What can be construed from that is if we allow the Lord to speak a true word through us, then the witness of Jesus will be present. That *witness*, meaning "evidence for," says that Jesus is inherent within the spirit of prophecy. Everything the Lord does and says is prophetic, and if we want to be His mouthpieces, we must let that spirit flow through us. That means that as we move in it, we line ourselves up with what the Lord is saying and doing *now*. And as we do that, we will be able to see how our alignment with Him flows further out on the horizon. We will begin to see where the Lord is going and what He wants to do.

We need to have a much higher perspective than WWJD ("What would Jesus do?"). I doubt that anyone on earth could possibly know what Jesus would do in every given situation. Our own opinions, lack of knowledge of the Scriptures and immature understanding of the Lord can lead to a faulty analysis. When Jesus was on earth, He said that He only did what He saw the Father doing (John 5:19). It was a moment-by-moment engaging in spiritual communication between Jesus and the Father. We will be totally ineffective in ministering if we do not do the same. What we

138

really need to know is WIJD (that is, "What *IS* Jesus doing?"). We need to know it moment by moment — not take "stabs," or "educated guesses," as to the Lord's intentions. We need to have the Word of God embedded in our spirits, but often situations call for a clear "now" word from Him about how He is moving. Daily obedience depends on it. That is the only way we will have the wisdom and strategy we need to defeat any foe.

When someone goes to a foreign country to minister, he or she will often use an interpreter to translate the message being preached into the native language as they preach. The same preacher could come across completely different depending on who the interpreter is. Some interpreters speak like a dictionary, translating word for word in a steady, monotone voice. If the interpreter's heart is not with the minister, much of his message can be lost. But if the interpreter takes hold of the message as it is spoken, he actually begins to preach the same words in his language under the very same anointing as the minister's. The interpreter may be listening closely to know what to say next, but he can also by his zeal, tone of voice and gestures, reach a point where it becomes difficult to tell who is the minister and who is the interpreter.

If we want to be true messengers of what the Lord wants to say in His church, we must be accurate in our interpretation of the language of the Spirit. We cannot just strive to be a prophetic dictionary; we need to be so close to Jesus that we are speaking His word with the timing and in the way He desires it to be spoken to His people. As His "interpreters," He wants us to flow and move just like He does, interpreting the word He puts in our spirits with human language that will convey the language of Heaven. As 1 Peter 4:11 says, *"If anyone speaks, let him speak as the oracles of God."*

The Lord wants to raise up men and women who will be like seashells in His church. When you hold a seashell up to your ear, you can "hear the sound of the ocean." God wants us to be a people who will draw others closer so that they can *hear the voice of God*. A seashell doesn't have a voice of its own; it can only amplify the sounds that flow through it. In the same way, we can only speak what the Lord speaks to us.

For a seashell to "sound like the sea," it must first be empty. The animal it once housed must leave. We, too, must become empty of the flesh for the Lord to sound clearly through us. The best thing about a seashell is that you can "hear the ocean" in it even if you're a thousand miles from the beach. Even if we are taken away from our desired habitats and are not close to where we think God is moving, we can still take the sound of His voice with us. We can speak His Word in the ear of someone who needs to hear His voice.

CHAPTER 16

THE GIFT OF HUNGER

*A*s I was praying one afternoon in May of 1989, the Lord spoke to me about some of the things He was going to do in the Body of Christ. This may not seem so amazing and unusual now; however, remember that the well-known renewal meetings of the nineties had not really begun to get under way. He began to speak to me of a new hunger that He was going to release on the Church. Of everything I wrote down that day, the following statements have always stayed with me:

> *"Those who see the Bridegroom will desire Him, and the passion of the Spirit shall be as none whom man has ever known. They will cry out for My presence even when I am yet upon them ...* **They will pray, 'It is not enough,' even though they would die if I came upon them any more ....**"

141

Obviously, the 1990's brought a surge of spiritual hunger to the Church. However, I know this word has not yet been fulfilled. I don't think we've reached the level where we have desperately prayed, "It is not enough" to the extent that we would literally die if the Lord's presence came any stronger upon us. I believe that kind of fervency can only happen if the Lord releases an insatiable hunger on His people. God can only release a greater anointing of His power as He grants us a greater capacity to receive it.

As we ask for the Lord to consume us with His presence, we need to realize the *source* of our hunger. It is only by God's mercy that we have the ability to reach for Him or desire Him. If there is a hunger in us for Him, it is not because of anything we have done. God Himself is the one who put it there. He is the one who gives us the *gift of hunger*.

When that greater capacity comes — by God's grace — anything lukewarm in us that has not been relinquished will try to smother that fire and keep us from that greater capacity God is trying to bring. Hunger is one of the best gifts God gives us to keep the lukewarm influence out of our hearts, so it must be guarded and nurtured.

Complacency kills spiritual hunger in a Christian. The two major instruments of complacency are *pride* and *discouragement*. Each injects the "victim" with a different kind of lukewarm poison. *Pride* will keep us self-sufficient, and that is dangerous because confessing need is the first key to spiritual hunger. As long as we are too proud to admit our need, we will never receive anything from the Lord.

Discouragement destroys our hunger because no matter how much we think that we love God, if we do not believe He is there for us, we will not pursue Him. Deep down, we may feel that He can't be trusted. If we have given up, we may not even be open to His overt attempts to comfort us. We may hang onto our discouragement, waiting for something encouraging to pull us out of it.

Discouragement makes us feel rejected, and we think the cure for rejection is finding acceptance. So we pray for God to demonstrate acceptance to us through redeemed circumstances or through favor with others. However, acceptance is not the answer. We are only setting ourselves up to be rejected again and again, requiring another dose of acceptance to cure us each time. *The ultimate remedy for rejection is not acceptance, but crucifixion.* If our flesh is crucified with Christ, rejection can't touch us.

I believe rejection is a major stronghold in the Body of Christ because it keeps us feeling unworthy to come into God's presence, and prevents spiritual hunger from soaking our hearts. (Yes, there are those who need prayer to be set free from rejection, and sometimes there is a necessary healing process to get over tragic abuses. So there is no condemnation here.) Our first step toward victory in this area is realizing that discouragement and rejection are tools of the enemy intended to bar us from spiritual fulfillment. Our desire for intimacy with the Lord must outweigh our perceived need to nurse our wounds. Let us not forget that Jesus faced the greatest rejection of all, and He commands us to take up our cross and follow Him. To move ahead with God, for some, may come down to a decision to let that rejection stay on the altar and die.

> *I have been crucified with Christ; it is no longer I who live, but Christ lives in me.*   Galatians 2:20

I have faced my share of rejection, and this has been a sensitive area for me. However, our identification with Christ guarantees that rejection will be a permanent part of a Christian's life. Once, while struggling with seemingly one rejection experience after another, I questioned the Lord about it. His lack of intervention was frustrating me! He gave me an instant perspective, however, with one statement. He said, "You will keep getting rejected until you don't care that you are rejected anymore." That is true crucifixion — being free from even *caring* that you are rejected. A crucified life leaves us surrendered completely to the Lord. Therefore, we become prime candidates for a relationship with Him that has no barriers and no limits.

In addition, hunger cannot stay genuine and wholly focused on God without holiness to temper it. Jesus promises in Matthew 5:6 that those who hunger and thirst for righteousness will be filled. The Lord gives us the gift of hunger so that we can seek His face and surrender ourselves to Him. Hunger provides tenacity in our seeking that we shouldn't waste. Rather, we should protect it as something precious.

Hunger also needs to be consistent. How healthy would you be if you became physically hungry only once a week? We need to whet our appetites and let our spiritual senses be enticed to wait on God. Many times, we seek to fill our spiritual hunger as though we are going to a restaurant and ordering what we like off the menu. Then, after the meal, we go home until the hunger pangs return. What we need to do instead is let our hunger take us to a higher level. We should seek God like we are going to one of those all-you-can-eat buffet places and let God fill us up. But we shouldn't just "eat and go home." No, we should *stay there*. The secret to staying hungry is to discipline yourself to *stay at the table*. Stay at that table, and never let your heart stray from Him. Stay in His presence. He honors that by giving you a bigger spiritual stomach. Your capacity will just grow and grow. Keep going back to that buffet and getting some more. Live at that table and eat of the Lord constantly. If you are determined to stay hungry, God will respond to that desire.

You may already consider yourself a hungry person, one who is pursuing God with all you have. You may even think you are the hungriest person you know. And you may be. But don't let that stop you from asking for a greater capacity and a greater hunger. The minute you think you are the hungriest saint who ever lived, you have begun to embrace the lukewarm spirit. Remember pride and lack of need? We even *need* God to make us hungry! We can never be hungry enough for God — never. Our goal should be to live hungry, even when we are congratulating ourselves for eating that fabulous buffet.

145

Seeking the fire of genuine hunger can be danger-ous. Hunger does not come without feeling empty and lacking, and there is a pain in it that can be excruciat-ing. When you are used to pleading, "Fill me," asking for emptiness is a very hard prayer. That's why luke-warm people will never pray for hunger. Leaving their comfort zone is out of the question. Your soul will rea-son with you to forget that and to just come and be filled, be joyous and be satisfied with the abundant fruit of the Lord. I'm not telling you to shun His bless-ings, but to ask for a lasting fruit of hunger that will carry you to and keep you at His feet.

There was a time in my life when I went through a very hurtful ministry situation. Through feelings of betrayal, anger and rejection, somehow I was given the grace to believe that "God meant it for good." Af-terward, I began to write down my thoughts. The Lord used this opportunity to show me how He'd made a major deposit in my heart:

The Father is in the Potter's house, crafting vessels at the wheel. He pauses from His work, His eye emanating power and creativity until it becomes full with an idea. He sud-denly swings around and takes a certain vase from the shelf and douses it with cupped handfuls of water. It begins to lose shape, and its texture becomes like raw clay again. He places the vase on the wheel and it turns. He gently guides it with His left hand, and His right hand pushes down firmly and deliberately into the vessel. The outside shape of the vase remains intact, but the inside has become hollowed out

—*fuller and deeper. The is clay stretched so much that the walls of the vase have become very thin. The vessel takes on a translucent nature and now looks very, very fragile.*

Lord, I have seen now where I have been, and what You have done in me. Just when I thought I knew my place on Your shelf, You whisked me away from comfort, familiarity and security. You poured things on me that I knew were of You, but it hurt because I began to lose My identity. Maybe You just never liked the way I looked. Was I a big mistake?

Then my whole world was spinning! I didn't feel that I belonged anywhere. I knew Your hand had not let go of me, but at the same time I felt violated. Where were all the moments of ecstasy I had felt in Your presence? I felt so much pain inside that I thought I would break. I became emptier and emptier, and life was pulled away from me into a darkness that was sure to overtake me.

Lord, I see now what You have done. You have pressed out areas where I was full of me, and have made more room for Yourself with the power of Your own hand. I am more fragile now and more vulnerable. But my dependence on You has increased, because I know if I fall now, I will not survive. I will be shattered to pieces. I know Your protection and strength alone will preserve me. I am not presumptuous enough anymore to take any leaps on my own.

You have not done this to make me feel better about myself or to make me more beautiful to others. In fact, I may look even worse for the wear and tear, but I am hollowed out and only You know how much more room there is inside of me for You now.

You wouldn't have taken me from the shelf had I not prayed for the end result. I do want to know You. But when purging came, I did not see past it. Somehow, there seems to be a moment of suffering that You require within a trial that involves a "free fall," at the very least. Is that why Jesus said, "Why have You forsaken Me?" When I felt forsaken, were You waiting to see if I would forsake You? Or were You trying to magnify my little speck of faith and devotion to You even when the whole universe was screaming that You are not God after all?

I am confronted with the new hollowness You have worked within me. I have finally discovered it is a precious gift. I thought I had sold it all to dig for You in the field! But all the while, You were digging out of me! You did all the work, and when You found enough emptiness, You left a treasure there. You left me a pearl of great price — hunger.

There's something I love about that greater empty place that You have given me, and I don't ever want it completely satisfied. I know now that I want to stay hungry more than I want to be filled. I never want to lose it. I would rather starve wanting You than feel that I am so filled up to the top that I could hold no more of You. When I feel that gnawing desire deep inside of me, I will remember Your loving hand pounding out that hidden place of glory within me. You saw what hunger I had as "hunger for hunger." You have credited what was perhaps nothing more than utter frustration as if it was a pure beseeching for a greater expanse of You in my life.

Touch me, Lord! But with the same insistence, I pray for the mercy to not grow weary of that touch. I know You have already carved a cleft in me that is reserved for You alone. Within the groanings of hunger in me, cause me to learn how to minister to You with it, and not just wallow in self-absorbed desire. Teach me how this passion can bring me closer to You. I don't want to just awkwardly run toward a distant finish. I pray that my vision will be as clear as the depth of the hunger I feel.

It is Your hand that has brought me here. I was feeling deserted, and I didn't see that You were hovering over me with Your most concentrated love. When I felt oppressed, now I know that my enemy stole nothing from me, but only drove me further into this place with You.

I know You have made me for Yourself, and I am honored to sit before You, hungering for Your presence.

Our ongoing hunger for God is dependent on our dependence. It is a gift we cannot manufacture on our own. We need to see our desire for Him as an acceptable, pleasing offering, not simply a deficiency that demands immediate relief. Our continual longing will only bring us closer to Him.

CHAPTER 17

PROVING GROUND

*I*n the Western world, we have been educated to believe that we must have evidence for everything. The validity of your convictions is judged by the strength of your argument. I think most of us have been frustrated at least once that God won't just answer by fire and "prove" Himself to the highly annoying skeptics or the secular media. Sometimes, it would be so nice to say, "There! See, we told you He is God!"

Just like the world, we in the Body of Christ have been seduced into wanting proof. We're not necessarily asking God to confirm His existence, but we have become so needy that many of us cannot take three steps forward without seventeen signs from Heaven. It's not just personal direction that we desire; we want constant assurances that He really does love us and that He knows our plight. We are insecure about His daily concern for us, so we often seek life-changing, tangible experiences from Him, just to make sure that He hasn't left the room or our lives. We hear about it happening to others, and we start to ask, "Why not me? Does the Lord play favorites?"

We wait for the Lord to spiritually charge us up so that it will be an exhilarating experience to run to the altar. We live for those moments of passion, when we say, "Yes, Lord," to anything and dance with all our might to prove it.

There is nothing wrong with wanting to be caught up in worship. Of course we love Him. What a wonderful blessing to be with Him. But for too many, when church is over, their flesh comes back with a vengeance to claim its uncrucified territory. Suddenly God is not meeting our criteria for us to praise or serve Him anymore — probably not until next week. The music is not playing, and we are not being romanced. In essence, we begin having one-night stands with Jesus, and we consider ourselves faithful because we claim that He is our only lover. *After all*, we think to ourselves, *it's not like we are going to other services and worshiping other gods!*

As the Scriptures are fulfilled, signs and wonders will become more commonplace. Even now, God is releasing tokens of His coming glory in the earth. In reading or hearing of these incidents, we must guard our hearts and realize that a degree of holy soberness must accompany any life-changing encounter with the Lord. Many notables who have had such tangible experiences weren't even praying for an experience, but they were dry, weak or frustrated with the shallowness of their ministries. They had simply come to the end of themselves and were desperate. They tied themselves to the altar, and God *did* answer by fire. Others have come along to reap the benefits of these ministries without realizing the prayer and spiritual desperation that preceded them.

Know this — that *every glorious manifestation is also the wrapping paper on a test*. Didn't Jesus show us that? He did great miracles, but He was always testing hearts to see if they would see past the manifestation and embrace the truth He was conveying. When He fed the multitudes, how many thought that the flavor of the bread was exceptional and were glad they got some free food? *Boy, that saved us a trip to McDonald's. Thank God. Not to mention the entertainment! What a magic show, watching bread multiply out of those baskets!* It was the first dinner theater! But what did the Lord want? He wanted the people to get a revelation of who He was — the Bread of Life. Did they want *bread* or *Bread*?

Are we panting as the deer for a mere crumb and missing the real Bread? Have we so deviated from our primary focus that we do not see that those things are not an end in themselves? Or do we just wait till the next time we are bothered by our distance from God, look up and say, "Thrill me"?

At the end of the day, the important question will be: What held the focus of our love and worship? Were we found worshiping our worthy Father alone, or did we turn our eyes to other things, even if they were manifestations or experiences that He Himself sent our way? We are often our own greatest stumblingblocks on the road to true revival. On one hand, we're praying for the Holy Spirit to do the miraculous. But if He graces us and meets our expectations, does He really want us to be so "wowed" and distracted by trinkets in the outer court that we don't go for the REAL treasure? We think we're pleasing the Lord with our hunger by saying, "Gimmee, gimmee." We keep asking for *more*. I think He's shaking His head at some of us, saying, "Well, more *what*?" It seems that some may get what they ask for but still miss Him altogether.

Every glorious manifestation is also the wrapping paper on a test. As we unwrap the manifestation and the pretty paper is discarded and we know it was really God and that He did move miraculously — then what? *Do we dare to cry out to Him passionately that we are awed by His power, but that's not what we're really after?* What?! In the midst of the most glorious, incredible thing we have ever seen, do we realize even then that we *still* don't really know Him and that we need *Him* desperately? Do we thank Him for His outpouring, but absolutely insist that we just want and need intimacy with Him all the more? How could we? Isn't that being ungrateful? Are we daring to cut off the hand of God from moving by seeking His face? Of course not. God just wants to know where our hearts are — that we desire Him above anything else. Ironically, this heart response from us would probably release the greatest spectrum of anointing and miracles imaginable! God can trust a people who are completely open to His power and surrendered to the moving of His Spirit, yet who remain focused on His face.

Some experiences produce eternal fruit, but in other cases, the highlight of an apparent manifestation of the Spirit is only a momentary high. It's not the minister's fault, and it's certainly not the Lord's fault. He is simply receiving a shallow response from a very shallow bride, and we fail to grasp the eternal significance of the gift He was trying to impart. And once again, we demonstrate how far we have to go. I am all for what *ignites* and deepens our faith, but sometimes we are more interested in what *excites* our faith. I have personally heard people ask earnestly for the latest thing God is doing, as it becomes a "sensation" and something to be coveted. Undoubtedly, many "get it," and I'm sure will rise to attest that their faith was increased and that they are closer to the Lord than ever before as a result of a manifestation.

That is a difficult argument to refute. But for myself, I will say that I'm just hard-pressed in praying for "something else." Someone may protest that I seem to be presenting an either/or proposition — that people choose either experiences *or* the deeper things of God. They may believe that I'm limiting Him. They may even say, "Hey, I can have it all — everything God has. I can be a deep Christian and still seek to experience the Lord in many ways." For me, all my desire is fixed in just one place, and, truthfully, that is so paramount in me that nothing else compares to it. Do I want spiritual experiences in my life? Yes! But in the comparison, why should I be spending a large percentage of my time asking for trivial, lesser things?

Just ask for *Him*. When you ask for *Him*, you *are*

asking for it *all* — but without losing your first desire. If visions and visitations come, so be it. And that is not a passive, "Okay, God, You know where I am. Go ahead if You want." A surrendered lover wouldn't have that attitude. It is a matter of focus and of where our ultimate expectations lie. Are we praying for a "what" or for a "Who"?

So, if our hearts are in the right place, and we are swept up in a wonderful experience, then what should our response be? Several years ago, I had a particularly life-changing experience with the Lord. During a week of special meetings at our church, the power of God began to move. The worship was intense, healings were taking place, and the presence of the Holy Spirit was strong. The pastor told everyone to join hands, and he walked down some of the aisles, touching the hand of the person on the end of each row. As he did, many of the rows of people were being slain in the Spirit — like dominoes. I happened to be on the end of my row, and he came by and touched my hand. Like most everyone, we all went down. After a while, the service continued, but I was still lying on the pew. I could not get up. The more I tried to get up, the deeper I fell into a state of spiritual bliss. I felt that I was aware of the rest of the service, yet later when I saw the video, incredibly, I had no recollection of most of what had transpired.

At the end of the service, the pastor told my husband that I would be in that state for the next twenty-four hours. My bewildered husband obediently carried me to the car, drove home, carried me into the house and put me on the bed. This is where I stayed, in my church dress clothes and unmoved, for the next twenty-four hours.

This became one of the most personal and intimate experiences I'd ever had with the Lord. To explain it now, I can only say that I deeply feel His presence, and my heart feels gripped and raw every time I remember it. In fact, I did not share about it publicly for eleven years. Even then, it was an extremely limited account, and I only did so out of clear direction from Him.

We all need to protect and preserve those secret things we have with the Lord, just as we would special intimacies about our marriages. When a person knows that his or her intimacy with you will be shared with others, there is a feeling of betrayal of that bond and a loss of intensity in the relationship. I feel the Lord wants to inhabit that secret place of trust and intimacy with us, yet we are too determined to go tell everybody about it. However, what happened in the aftermath of my experience does give me something constructive that I can pass on to you.

The prophesied "twenty-four hours" was still not over when the next night's service began. My husband left me home, still in my "state," and our pastor asked him to share what had happened to me. Our friends who owned a local Christian television station wanted to interview me on the air and had already been talking about the event on their flagship program that day. Other people prayed for the Lord to give them the same experience. By the time I finally came back to church on the third evening of the meetings, I was treated with a sense of awe by some, and several people asked me if they could touch me. I felt like Moses coming down from the mountain. I was amazed at the hunger in these people, even though it was misdirected at me and expressed immaturely.

I refused to give any public explanation, and quietly withdrew from any attention. I knew that my experience had been a precious gift from the Lord, and I was going to keep it undefiled. If there was one message I *could* have given during that time, it would have been that the experience itself was purely a gift of concentrated intimacy. I had been continually hungry for the Lord and sought after an ever-deepening relationship with Him. I never asked for "an experience." I asked for *Him*, and that is one way He chose to answer my heart's desire. What happened to me was something that I would never have thought to ask for. I was busy with the daily demands of caring for a husband and five young children. God must have chuckled as He thought of a creative way for me to have some very quality time with Him. It completely changed my life and intensified my relationship with Him. But it was all about His presence and the intimacy that resulted. He just poured so much of Himself on me at once that I was overcome by it in a way that made an eternal imprint on my life.

It's all about *Him*. The person of Jesus. That day, He became *very* real to me. If you ever get a good look at Him, I guarantee that you will never again care if you ever see an angel or a cloud. I'm cured — I will always desperately seek to know Him more within any experience that comes my way. I know that the Lord has a purpose when He allows or gives those things, and I don't dismiss them — but I want to see Jesus. Even when He sends a supernatural experience, He wants us to see past it. He's testing our hearts. These things can point to the Lord, but they are not Him, and they do not adequately portray His overwhelming beauty by any means. He is so much more beautiful. We have not even begun to see the glory of God. As tremendous as my experience was, I do not ask Him to repeat what He did. God has done other incredible things since then, but when He does, I set my sights high on His face. It's not something I have to struggle to remind myself to do. Ironically, it takes less for me to see His hand now than it did before.

I am sincerely greedy for *eternal fruit*, even if someone only lays hands on me with a short prayer. If the anointing of the Lord is present, that means He is at work. He is doing something in my life, and I want to hold on to anything He would want to say to me or impart to my spirit. Most of what the Lord does in my life comes in simple ways, not the miraculous. If it had to be a laser light show to be God, I would miss out on much of what He wants to give me. I am convinced that He will continue to answer my heart's cry with greater things than I could conceive of anyway. So He's in charge of that. We all need to get spoiled on Jesus. Nothing will kill that lukewarm monster in us faster than saying, "It takes *Him* to satisfy me, and I just won't settle for anything else."

CHAPTER 18

A CALL TO UNBRIDLED PASSION

*T*he Lord desires that His children walk in a passion for Him that is *free from restraint*. However, as a result of the mounting fear of "getting in the flesh," some hesitate in allowing the Lord complete liberty to touch them because of real or perceived abuses they may have seen in the church.

Whatever a person's response to the Lord — from the stone-faced, to those in an exaggerated display, to anything in between — none of us are immune from getting in the flesh. Being in the flesh is simply failing to submit ourselves completely to the Lord, whether we are blatantly resisting Him or creating a man-made distraction.

When we are no longer under subjection to the Holy Spirit, we are in error — regardless of the excesses we might fear. One of the fruits of the Spirit is self-control, but that fruit does not apply to our passion for the Lord. We exhibit the fruit of self-control when we draw upon the Holy Spirit to crucify our flesh and sinful nature, but it is not an excuse to keep an extravagant love for the Lord in check. When Mary of Bethany anointed the feet of Jesus, she was criticized for her lavish "waste" of perfume, and one can assume that her shameless display was socially embarrassing for everyone in the room. David danced with joy before the ark through the streets of Jerusalem, to the total horror of his wife Michal. The Scriptures tell us of her sharp rebuke, but the reactions of other people are not given. It is quite possible that others agreed with Michal but exercised more wisdom by not criticizing their king to his face!

Confusion in the Body of Christ over what is acceptable and "in order" stems from the fact that we must know His voice and His ways before we ever enter into a questionable situation. If we are filled with an intimate knowledge of Him, we will have the discernment necessary to know if *He* is the Spirit behind what is happening in a church service.

For example, I know my husband very well and I know that he would not rob a bank or go drinking at a bar. Even his remote acquaintances would know that too. I know what his favorite foods are, but his close friends have also figured that out from spending time with him. There are some things, though, that only I know about him — things only a wife could know. After many years of marriage, I often know what he is going to say before he says it. At times, I even feel as though I am preaching his sermons with him. Unfortunately, most Christians only have the kind of relationship with Jesus where they know that He would not rob a bank. When they get into a situation that is not as clearly black or white, they are incapable of discerning the true fingerprint of God.

Until we know the Lord to the extent that we can determine His presence in most situations, we need to pray for Him to bring wise ones alongside us who will point the way and help us to grow into maturity. Likewise, our heart for the Lord can always be a compass pointed in the right general direction if we walk in continued surrender to Him. The Holy Spirit will still guide us and give us discernment if we will ask Him. He will then refine our spiritual senses as we get to know Him better. Our degree of submission to the Lord is infinitely more important than how we might define "maturity."

In the "divorce" that we try to create between flesh and spirit, our emotions are the "child" caught in the middle of the custody battle. Like the lawyer who argues that children are better off with their nurturing mother, our spirit often automatically decides that our emotions will be better off "living with" the flesh. That way, our spiritual side can make a clean break and be free from childish emotions. But how can you *love the Lord your God with all your heart, with all your soul, and with all your strength* (Deuteronomy 6:5) without emotions and feelings? Even God expresses emotions, such as anger, sadness, love, and hatred for His enemies. For some reason, we have been led to believe that being emotionless is being "holy." Because of the way Jesus has been portrayed many times in film by those who don't even know Him, we may have a hard time imagining our "formal" and "stoic" Lord weeping at the tomb of Lazarus, or truly believing that He was actually *"anointed ... with the oil of gladness more than [His] companions"* (Psalm 45:7). Jesus was full of joy, and there was even a heavenly *anointing* of rejoicing on Him! We need to give our emotions completely over to the Lord so that He can use them as He wills for His pleasure and glory, trusting that He will prune out what is not acceptable to Him. If we can only know His desire for us to completely surrender to Him ... .

"You are like the driver of your own stagecoach, holding the reins to Your passions. You are equipped with a team of two healthy and strong horses — on the left, a dark one, representing the desires derived from your soulish nature, and on the right, a white one, representing your passion for Me and My ways.

"You have thought, I must bridle these two horses and hold the reins equally. I can't let them take me where I don't want to go, or let them gallop too fast.

"You have opted for restraint and self-control over your worldly passions. But why do you bridle My beautiful white horse? Why are you afraid of your passion for Me?

"Remove the bit from the mouth of the white horse; it grieves My Spirit. If you will remove it, then you will hear My voice clearly. Loosen your grip from his reins. DO NOT SAY 'WHOA' TO ME. Do not say, 'No, not this way, Lord.

I'm scared. This is not what I expected.' Don't be bound to the control and security you feel as the driver, 'balancing' your worldly passions with your godly passions, making them march perfectly in step together and having a parade!

"It's time to let go of the white horse! That's right — let the white horse run wild. If you let it rule, your right hand will then be filled with the authority of My strength and the wisdom of My Spirit. He will lead, and your heart will dance in a new freedom.

"As much as you feared loss of control, to your surprise, the dark horse will actually begin to realize he is overpowered. He was once haughty and self-important, because you had always equally yoked him with the white horse. But now, he will cower, knowing he will be unmercifully dragged in whatever direction the white horse chooses if he does not submit. The flesh must bow to the Spirit.

"You will always have the reins. You can slow Me down — but please don't, for I am leading you rapidly and wildly to a place of unbridled passion for Me! As you relinquish your restraint, the dark horse will try to convince you that he will buck and tear you away with ungodly reckless abandon. This is not so. Don't be tempted again to keep the two horses yoked neck and neck.

"So, release my wonderful, beautiful horse that will steal you away, My bride! Don't you see, I haven't wanted mere consent! I don't want a voluntary but timid bride who only loves Me in the most trivial way. I don't want a bride who will be afraid of Me on our wedding night and who just feels caught in a state of obligation for the sake of obedience. I want a bride so in love, so all-consumed in her thoughts of Me, that she is determined and deliberate about throwing away that bridle!

"Reject those things that would entice you to pull the reins back, that would stop this momentum I have stirred up in you. If you will forsake the 'l', the 'lukewarm', and let Me burn it out, then there will no longer be a b-r-i-d-l-e; only you, My b-r-i-d-e. There will be no more restraints and nothing between us.

"Commit yourself to My unrelenting passion. Let go. I am enough for your inadequacies, and your dependence on Me should be complete. But I will not—no, I cannot—fill you with surrender or impose on you a desire toward Me. I can draw you, but you must respond, so that I can come and build on that foundation of love a temple beyond your ability to love Me on your own.

"Do you dare trust Me with your spiritual passion? How tight your grip has been on those reins! My sweet bride, your desire for a so-called 'acceptable' appearance before the world has hurt Me. It's only you and Me in the chambers, and these layers of elegant 'coverings' are not appropriate. I want to be close to you, but I will not kiss you through your veils of propriety and piety. The enemy would be pleased if you would hesitate toward Me — even out of respect and reverence. But there is no shame in unrestrained, holy intimacy with Me!

"I will not come until My bride is ready. But her expectancy and purity is not enough. Prayerfulness and obedience is not even good enough! I am pouring My passion for My bride on My Church, but how much is spilling off cold hearts? My sweet words and My most *intimate love songs are unrequited. How often is even My simple touch rejected? I am repeatedly relegated to the back of the line — behind her many other pursuant suitors.*

"But, oh, I will wait! I will! For Me, there is only only one bride, only one marriage! I will see her full of the passion I desire before I come. I am patient and loving, and the ravishing she will ravish Me with will be worth the wait. She is lovely! And I will continue to pour and pour and pour until she can resist Me no more!"

As we unbridle our passion for God, He will release us from those things that have kept us from true fulfillment and intimacy with Him. As beautiful as Heaven will be, Jesus offers us a prenuptial taste of His wonderful love here and now.

Chapter 19

Wood for Fire

roverbs 26:20 says, *"Where there is no wood, the fire goes out."* We, as the "trees of the Lord," are the only source of fuel He can use to kindle a fire in Laodicea. Therefore, we must be willing kindling so that His fire is kept ablaze. The Holy Spirit is stirring up a repulsion for the effects of the lukewarm spirit that mirrors the Lord's own grief. Disgust for all Laodicea represents must increase significantly before it will be expelled from our churches. We must determine to have zero tolerance for it in our own lives.

Some of you are little flickers that have been lit in Laodicea. You feel quite small and obscure. You've been frustrated, and you've been thinking, *It must be just me.* Although it may not be apparent to you, that obscurity does not prevent the Lord from using your fervor to illumine the passivity around you. The identification you feel with the rejected and the misunderstood will foster a godly humility in your life and yield a brighter flame.

You will find your desire for emptiness overtaking your desire for fullness. You will be able to see the contrast of vanity to true value. This will compel you to pursue an absolute availability to the Holy Spirit.

Many are confused about who they are in the Body of Christ. They don't know if they are a hand or foot. Even if they did know, they still wouldn't know *where* to fit in. The Lord longs for His Church to be perfected, but those spots and wrinkles will be purged from the inside out. Those who answer the call to be flames in dark places will be part of the true heart of His bride. You might be hidden, but your strength is crucial to the life flowing in His Church.

You may feel like a tiny flame in danger of being snuffed out. You might wish that you could be part of a bigger, raging fire so you could stay confidently ignited when you get weary. But remember, big fires can get out of control and consume not only what needs to be burned, but everything else in their paths. The Lord does not want a wildfire: He wants a blaze that is useful and that will be subject to the direction of the Holy Spirit.

The Lord has a certain pattern and shape in mind for His fire. If you can imagine the globe of the earth with little lights strategically placed at different intervals — that is how the Lord is working out the order of His plan. Links of flames and various patterns will emerge as He connects it all together intricately as a functional fire ablaze with His glory.

As we all face our own plight in Laodicea, we must be mindful of the fact that we are called to something much larger, as the Body and the bride of Christ. Even though we may not always be where we would like to be, we must look at the plan of God as a whole and have faith that we have a destiny to see the Kingdom established.

If we become downhearted, we may give up before the fruit comes to full harvest. We cannot command even what we ourselves have sown and watered to bud when we want it to, because only the Lord knows the time of harvest. We need to trust that He will be the Lord of that harvest.

God has extended grace to many believers in extenuating circumstances. Just because you are not a martyr or a missionary in a pagan country does not mean that you are undeserving of His protection in the same way. The Lord knows who the overcomers are. All who overcome will do so only because they have leaned on Him — whatever their circumstances.

We are meant to operate as a body, so it is good to keep in mind that God will only grant a measure of sufficiency to us that is in keeping with His blueprint for the Church. That is to say, He will not let you isolate yourself on a desert island, then grace you with the ability to operate in all the gifts so that you can minister to yourself. If we are not spiritually or geographically connected to a nurturing body of believers, God does preserve us, but we will never thrive as we would if we were in a situation where we were receiving the fullness of scriptural equipping. For this reason, we should be open to changes the Lord would want to make in our locations and vocations. If we are patient until we see the roadmap of God's clear direction, then His wisdom and peace will lead us into the provision we have asked of Him.

Having made the decision to follow Jesus, we still have another choice to make. We have to decide *HOW* we will follow Jesus. The results of that decision may not determine our eternal home, but it can alter our destinies considerably. After being redeemed and coming out of the cold, will we only go halfway, to that lukewarm place of religious rhetoric and moral striving? Will we offer the King of Kings nothing more than a small token of "flippant worship," and give our Bridegroom only a passing glance?

The Lord wants to be our sole passion. His heart longs for us to come to Him in a fervent devotion. He wants to see our reservations burned to ashes and a continual hunger for Him. *With His abundant love, He is calling our hearts to leave Laodicea.*

Until My Heart Leaves Laodicea

Take me to the fervent fire
Where all my flesh must die.
I'm pleading for Your righteousness,
For I am broken, poor, and blind.

Until my heart leaves Laodicea,
Melt my richest dross away.
Lord, my zeal clings to Your altar
Until my heart leaves Laodicea.

The hottest oil has filled my eyes
And left me starving for
The feast of seeing face-to-face
The Voice behind the door.

Until my heart leaves Laodicea,
Melt my richest dross away.
Lord, my zeal clings to Your altar
Until my heart leaves Laodicea.

You have no part of lukewarm hearts
That beat with complacency,
So take the branding iron of love's desire
And burn it into me.

Until my heart leaves Laodicea,
Melt my richest dross away.
Lord, my zeal clings to Your altar
Until my heart leaves Laodicea.

ABOUT THE AUTHOR

Jeanne Terrell has a pastoral and prophetic ministry with her husband, Kim. Their primary focus is on hunger for God, holiness, and the fear of the Lord. Jeanne also has a burden for intercessory prayer, worship and personal ministry, imparting vision and equipping others to fulfill their highest calling in Christ.

Jeanne and Kim have five children — Julie (happily married to Donny), Kevin, Jill, Keith and Kyle.

Jeanne can be contacted in care of the publisher:

McDougal Publishing
PO Box 3595
Hagerstown, MD 21742.

or through e-mail at LeavingLaodicea@aol.com.